just give me the road

anne marie romer

Cover design: Brandie Grogan

Printed in the United States of America
Published by Braughler Books LLC., Springboro, Ohio

First printing, 2020

ISBN: 978-1-970063-48-6

Library of Congress Control Number: 2019920553

Ordering information: Special discounts are available on quantity purchases by bookstores, corporations, associations, and others. For details, contact the publisher at:

    sales@braughlerbooks.com

    or at 937-58-BOOKS

For questions or comments about this book, please write to:

    info@braughlerbooks.com

Braughler™
Books
braughlerbooks.com

For Phil.
Supporting every word of this story is his
steady and strong presence for his family.
He has always been my sister's greatest gift.

A sister can be seen as someone who is both ourselves
and very much not ourselves
—a special kind of double.

Toni Morrison

the road to chicago

☙ chapter 1 ☙

Just past the midnight hour on Sunday, March 17, 2013, the doorbell rang in frantic repetition causing our two dogs to yelp with alarm. My husband, Mark, quickly rose from bed to investigate. The antennas of worry cultivated over years of motherhood heightened. Having teenagers does that. From my bed, I could see through the windows into our family room as lights turned on. I remained curious, waiting for Mark to return—annoyed at the inconvenience of being awakened. Then I saw Jack, my 16-year-old nephew, sitting on the couch. His head was buried in his hands. I was puzzled, fearing something was very wrong. A foreboding chill seized me with looming alarm. I froze.

"Anne," I heard Mark yell down the hall, "Conor's been in an accident." The pit in my stomach exploded with fear. I rose to meet the darkness of this night. There would be no turning back.

Jack didn't know many details; only that his brother, Conor was on his way to a Chicago hospital. He reported that my sister, Kathy, and her husband Phil, received some kind of emergency phone call, and subsequently left by car for the five-hour drive to be with their oldest son. Kathy instructed Jack to come to our house so as not to be alone. Considering how much our family lives were intertwined; our children were quite familiar with the route between our homes. I could feel Jack's anxiety as he swayed back and forth on our couch, trying to keep the rise

3

of panic at bay. Already this did not feel like a minor accident. Anxiety took hold of my shallowing breath. Conor was 18, a freshman at Loyola University in Chicago, and the second of my sister's three children. He was a rising star in the world, poised for greatness. His academic successes, athletic abilities, personality charm, and humility proceeded him in all things. Some kids have a worry-free guarantee—Conor was one of them.

Just hours earlier, Jack, the youngest of Kathy's three children, attended a high school dance enveloped in the frivolity of teenage fun. Shared silliness with friends, goofy dance moves, and late-night milkshakes were now a distant memory as he sat hugging himself; corralling his alarm.

I called my sister, hoping to hear a report that was contrary to Jack's demeanor. She answered her cell phone but was reluctant to talk as she expected a phone call from a hospital representative with an update on Conor's condition. Her report was curt. They'd received a call just short of midnight from a crisis care manager at the Advocate Illinois Masonic Hospital in Chicago. Although details were sketchy, Conor had been hit by a car while walking in a crosswalk just before midnight. He'd been transferred by ambulance to the emergency room where a trauma team awaited his arrival. His condition was serious. Kathy's voice was deliberate. I heard her call to bravery.

The severed connection left me longing to be with her. I envisioned my brother-in-law gripping the steering wheel, his white knuckles and lead foot willing the car beyond the 70-miles-an-hour speed limit. The distance between them and their son must have felt colossal. I was certain this night felt like an eternity. I thought of Kathy, staring out the passenger window to the nothingness of darkness, clutching her cell phone. I sensed her terror, but even in these initial moments of trying to place her mounting worry, I was heartened by the tone of her voice. Her words were grounded in the belief that Conor would be okay, that somehow his young life prepared him for this, and that she would see him through. All they could do was wait, and drive, and wait.

"We just need to get there," she'd said to me, "but I know in my heart he'll be okay."

Kathy's choice to lead with love navigated their journey to Conor's side, but I also felt a looming tsunami of fright. I could only hope the reality didn't meet the underlying dread.

My son Ben, a medical student at The Ohio State University, was in Chicago the night of Conor's accident. Following an urgent call from Kathy, he made his way to Advocate Illinois Masonic Hospital. Kathy entrusted Ben to help communicate with the medical team. Joining Ben were my niece Megan (a resident of Chicago) and Conor's best friend, Keenan Plate, who kept an anxious vigil in the surgical intensive care unit (SICU) waiting room until Kathy and Phil arrived.

I called Ben, hoping for reassurance that Conor's condition wasn't as bad as we suspected. His voice cracked amid the growing intensity of the situation. I heard uncharacteristic hysteria in his voice. "Neurosurgeon…central line…trauma team…" His medical understanding morphed into fear, and he began to weep. His alarm terrified me.

"I don't know, Mom. I don't know if he's okay."

The pause between minutes seemed like an eternity as we waited for additional word from Chicago. Jack, however, needed me to be present. We encouraged him to remain hopeful. I rubbed his back, hoping the rhythmic touch would calm his fraying nerves. I sent him upstairs and suggested he try to sleep in anticipation of what the morning would bring. I returned to bed, reaching into the drawer of my bedside table for the rosary my mom had given me years before. My fingers kneaded the square-shaped beads. I began a litany of Hail Marys, one after the other—aloud, so my fear could be managed by the sound of my voice in rhythmic prayer. My husband paced the floor, hands resting on the small of his back. "Come on, Conorman. Come on, Conorman," he repeated to the heavens. As a physician, he knew the graveness of the situation, as did Ben. I was slower in understanding, preferring to rest in denial. Surely this couldn't be that bad.

Terror festers in the dark. The hours till daylight were long and full of helpless energy. Like a locomotive, fear and dread gained momentum as I tried to remain centered. I pleaded to God and the entire scope of the heavens.

"Please," I said over and over. "Please take care of him."

One prayer after another moved the remainder of the night toward day, wishing the news from Chicago would not mirror my quickening heartbeat. I longed to be at my sister's side. We were used to navigating life's challenges together. Sharing burdens was made easier because we took turns supporting one another, making sure the way through difficulty was done hand in hand. Already, though, this was different. This time, Kathy and Phil shared the lone heartache of their child in need. This would not be the last time I felt helpless and inadequate in my love for her. Still, I yearned to be at her side.

The sun rose, bringing light to the increasing seriousness of Conor's injury. Kathy and Phil had arrived at the hospital at 3 a.m., coatless, wearing yesterday's clothes and slippers. The first person they saw upon entering the emergency room was Fr. Patrick Dorsey, a chaplain from Loyola who was "on call" for student emergencies requiring pastoral intervention. From the outset, Loyola embraced the opportunity to help care for the peripheral needs of the Crippen family. Conor was one of theirs, and this Jesuit community's dedication to his healing would be evident in the hours, days, weeks, and months to come.

Upon introduction to Fr. Patrick, Kathy and Phil looked at one another, believing somehow my brother Pat was present from his heavenly perch, giving an initial indication that Conor would be okay. It's all about perspective and choice, perhaps; and although there are skeptics who hesitate to attach spiritual meaning to randomness, the belief that God lived in the details of this journey was supported through Fr. Patrick. He would become my sister's spiritual guide throughout Conor's recovery journey in Chicago. And it worked for me to think our Pat was finding his way to be with her.

Kathy and Phil were taken to the family waiting room just outside the SICU on the fourth floor. They were given a report on Conor's condition, of which Kathy heard nothing. Her need to see Conor deafened her ability to hear. She found a nearby sink and brought handfuls of water to her parched mouth, seeking strength. It was time to find her son.

✦ chapter 2 ✦

When two sets of eyes born from the same cloth see a sunset, one view might be drawn to the upward sky, where the sun's encore performance paints the heavens with dazing brushstrokes of orange and violet. Another observation might rest on the horizon as the fading sun melts along the earth's edge, leaving a postscript of explosive grandeur and radiance. Contrasting perspectives of the same viewpoint define sisterhood. My sister, Kathy and I are no different. We fit the stereotypes of oldest versus youngest. Six years older, I take charge. Kathy accepts the flow. I have skirts in my closet from 20 years ago, Kathy welcomes a seasonal wardrobe refurbish in step with the latest color schemes and trends. I'm the one laughing while Kathy jokes. My sister is funny, and I'm her best audience. Kathy is unabashed in her emotional honesty and fosters connections with others through her acceptance and embrace of all things different. She is like the bright, colorful silk scarf wrapped loosely around your neck, where soft and yummy comfort meets bold style.

Kathy taught me the power of red lipstick, saying a woman needs to be daring. She counseled me not to worry when my daughter dyed her hair pink. I encouraged her to tend to herself the way she cared for others. When I urged her to try on the blue fringe dress with matching floral satin shoes, it came along with the reminder that it's all about price per wear. It's since become a staple in her closet. During the years when she felt worn from balancing home life with her teaching career, my offer of a good book was a passive aggressive way of telling her it was okay to sit with a cup of hot tea on a Sunday afternoon in self-indulgence. Who else but your best-friend sister could know what you mean when you say, "You know, that actress who won the Academy Award and looks really good in green?"

"Oh yeah," my sister replied, "you mean Julianne Moore."

Kathy is the one who took my then teen-aged daughter, Kate, to a coffee shop to talk about how all of us need to hold ourselves in the highest esteem. Soon after, my daughter dumped the not-so-great boyfriend. While on a road trip along I-75, I took the "being stuck in the car" opportunity to intervene with Kathy's daughter, Bridget, regarding her potential in the academic world and that she should never sell herself short. Now, she's preparing to graduate with a doctorate degree. Kathy and I are a force made stronger by our bond. We understand the backstories that define our lives, our children's lives, and know without words the state of our hearts. We love one another completely, laugh together incessantly, and talk several times a day. Indeed, we are a special kind of double. One of the reasons we love our husbands so much is that they are well aware and fully accept that when Kathy and I refer to "my sister," we are speaking about the other half of our soul.

Several family factors contributed to our closeness. Among them was the fate of our sibling birth order: three brothers, then two sisters. Pat was the oldest, and Neil and Gerry followed. Three years separate Gerry and me. For a long time, connection with him provided the soft place for my heart to rest. I shared a bedroom with Gerry for six years until Kathy was born. His steady presence disarmed the monsters of my bad dreams with silliness and banter. He made me laugh all the time, but still I felt lost amidst the big-brother world of Sunday afternoon football and balled-up athletic socks. I longed for an ally—someone whose hair I could brush into a bow-decorated ponytail. It felt like we waited forever for my sister, and her entrance into our world followed painful loss. Kathy came along following the stillbirth of a full-term son, Thomas. Yearning for another baby was the antidote to my mother's grief. She had a special place in her heart my sister. We all did. For me, she was the answer to prayer. Because of the gender-clumped grouping, my siblings and I were referred to as "the boys" and "the girls."

We seemed to do family pretty well. As a little girl, I skipped in happiness, feeling the world was defined by butterflies and dandelions. My mom's bedtime stories—where colors came to life—and Friday morning trips to the grocery store for Coke and potato chips left imprints of love that paved the path of my earliest years. My mom wasn't a very good cook and our dishes and silverware were mismatched, but her commitment to family cohesiveness blanketed us all. She manifested her commitment to loyalty by insisting that dinnertime was non-negotiable and reminding us of how precious siblings bonds could be. Her experiences as a child left her with an unyielding mission to cultivate family cohesiveness—something she'd always longed for.

A product of Irish immigrants, my mom was adopted at the age of 5 by an affluent couple in New York City. She never knew why she was given away by her birth mother, but the story of being unwanted germinated from an early age. Her upbringing was defined by a jealous and often mean-spirited adoptive mother whose own life left her incapable of showing consistent affection and acceptance. My mom was sent away to a Catholic boarding school in upstate New York shortly following her adoption.

Carrying the burden of feeling unloved as a child left a wound hard to heal.

In the absence of siblings, my mom was forced to rely on her own imagination for companionship. She recalled lying in bed as a child, picturing her birth parents as part of a greater story involving the kind of love that justified giving her away. Somewhere in her dreams lived a family where she was remembered and missed. Maybe this is where her uncanny capacity to find good in everything was born.

Despite her troubled childhood, my mom was able to bring forth the unconditional ability to love her own children. Consistently, the delight we saw on her face when she looked at us was, I think, the greatest gift a mother can give a child. Whether she cared for us when we were sick, packed our lunches with a special love note, told us a nap would make all things better, or made us stay in our rooms between noon and 3:00 pm on Good Friday, her imprint was always love-driven. Even my straight "C" report card was met with reassuring hugs and belief in my obscured potential.

"Pick a color," my mom used to say as she tucked me into bed each night. And just like that, orange castles, pink frogs, or green princesses would flood my sleepy mind, offering dreams of imagination and splendor. Eventually, her grandchildren benefited from "Gigi's" imagination and willingness to take the time to snuggle. My mom was able to fill the brokenness of her childhood with vibrant tales of goodness.

Following Jack's birth, my mom assumed the role of caregiver for my sister's kids. The opportunity for her to be intimately involved with them yielded pretty special relationships. Yes, Gigi was annoying when she insisted Jack wear his coat outside even as the warm March air suggested coats were no longer necessary.

Bridget would tell you that as a young child, the fact that Conor was allowed to cheat at Monopoly was quite irritating especially when Bridget owned Boardwalk and Park Place. Yes, they rolled their eyes, but my mom was on the floor with them all the time, playing to their hearts' content. They played games, did puzzles, and sang songs. Gigi, too, frolicked on the backyard swing set. Bridget's fascination with reading was born from their trips to the library. My mom came to know Jack's heart and his capacity for compassion and service. Hence, her characterization of him as a "peace-maker" stuck and was encouraged throughout his formative years. Each morning Conor and my mom would have Cheerio races to see who could slurp up all the floating "O's" first. It didn't matter that milk dripped from their chins or splashed beyond their bowls. Laughter and delight reigned. Conor did seem to win every time at game playing. For my mom, winning was overrated. Even during the epic games of Risk where the goal was to conquer the world, my mom would choose to control Luxembourg; the smallest country with the smallest army.

The quality of time Bridget, Conor, and Jack had with my mom engraved their hearts with deep affection for her. As age and illness debilitated her ability to get out, her grandchildren came to her. On those afternoons when Conor would stop by with an iced tea from Wendy's, my mom wished to know all things new. Conor talked about what he'd recently learned in school or through his curiosities. He made her laugh by recounting silly stories. He gave her the gift of time. She listened, and then she would throw her arms up in the air and remind Conor how gifted he was. Before his high school dances, Conor brought his date over so Gigi could delight in how handsome he was and how beautiful his date looked. Their bond was tight. My mom's death the year before Conor's accident spared her from the heartache of his injury. I'm not sure how she could have handled the helplessness in knowing he was so gravely hurt. The tenderness and purity of her grandmother love would have left her with unimaginable grief. We were consoled by the fact that her passing spared her from such pain, but found solace in our belief that love transcended earthly barriers. Her love for Conor was just too grand.

Those fortunate enough to know my mom felt her optimism, joy, and her untiring ability to put love before all else. She exuded infectious warmth. At times her need for love born from embedded insecurities felt onerous, but the light in her eyes and brilliance of her smile reflected the beauty of her essence—ultimately outweighed the burden of her need. Our mom was remarkable. And her grip…well, there was no one who could squeeze strength like she did.

I often wonder how my mom and dad came to marry. I believe her attraction had nothing to do with my dad and everything to do with his family. A musical crew, the Grogans gathered regularly, sharing picnic meals and engaging in sing-alongs around the old upright piano. The chaos, shared laughter, and community born from learned lyrics was intoxicating for my mom. Belonging to family provided a huge tent of security for her; my mom wanted nothing more than to be enveloped in kinship. It's silly for me to wish she hadn't married my dad, for that would have negated our whole story. But my heart does break for the 21-year-old vibrant girl who became my mom. I think she compromised herself and the potential for marital happiness for the cloak of family, and in doing so, set herself up for years of heartache.

My dad was the quintessential entertainer, playing the piano and charming anyone in the room with his sing-along style.

He was also a compulsive gambler, and over years, racked up thousands of dollars in debt. The obligation to pay financial liabilities undoubtedly fell to my mom to settle. I think about her trip to the local pawn shop when she hawked her engagement ring. I think about her embarrassment and anguish when creditors called demanding due loan payments. These were the days when a woman was defined by her husband's assets and had no legal right to independent ownership. My mom had no other choice than to carry his financial burdens. I think about the repetitive cycle of addiction and how that not only fueled toxicity and anger, but facilitated shame born from secrets. I never remember tenderness between them, even their twin beds screamed distance. Venom-filled conversations were the norm. Simple discussions dripped with bile of unresolved anger. Their marriage was a dysfunctional mess.

My brothers, in their adolescences, absorbed the strain of my dad's inability to man-up. Pat, Neil, and Gerry spent their teen-aged years trying to reconcile an inept father and a burdened mother. Gerry recalls as a young teen peeking into our darkened kitchen as my mom sat in solitude in the midnight hours, chain-smoking her way through worry. Detachment and perceived indifference towards his children left my brothers with layers of resentment toward my dad, where the only option for relief came from leaving. For years, I wondered if the burial of these family skeletons contributed to my brothers' eventual demise.

Despite the undertones of family imperfections, my childhood memories were happy and filled with laughter. We had an unrelenting ability to find humor in everything. Giddiness and hilarity were constant and cathartic. Teasing and fun at our own expense became our family remedy to stress. The table where my mom negotiated her burdens with late-night coffee and cigarettes was the same that offered the ability to reset our suppressed pain with levity and merriment at dinnertime.

Neil assumed the role of family clown and provided comic relief in response to submerged tensions which tended to bubble up as we all sat around the table. Slapstick-style fun where mashed potatoes ended up on his forehead, or where shifting eyes pointed to my dad's annoying way of chewing left us collapsed in stifled giggles. God forbid my dad caught us in amusement. His verbal anger outbursts in response to our dinnertime antics made us all cringe. Often, we couldn't dodge his ire, but it didn't matter. It just felt good to laugh. I smile even now thinking about those times my mom would say, "This is the first time I've laughed all day."

In later times of loss or stress, my family's therapeutic need to find humor in the most tragic circumstances was often misunderstood by those who would come to pay respects. Whether sitting in hospital rooms teasing with self-deprecating banter, holding vigil as our mom transitioned between life and death, or trying to comprehend inexplicable loss, we nestled together in laughter. This was our Grogan brand of bonding, which allowed us to convey a steadfast expression of loyalty.

Eventually, our family unit dissipated. My dad left. Pat got married. Neil became a traveling salesman, and Gerry left for college. This left a truncated family of a mom and her two girls, and it became our new normal. My mom immersed herself deeper and deeper into the lives of Kathy and me, and we came to depend on one another to share the responsibilities of loving her. Disenchanted in marriage and with minimal social connections, her heart yearned for a happiness found in forever-after novels. She lived vicariously through Kathy and me, reveling in our high school sweetheart relationships with young men who would later become our husbands. The joys and opportunities of her daughters made up for those she had longed for as a young woman.

My dad was gone for nearly 20 years. Really, it was like he went out for a gallon of milk and just didn't come home; abandoning his family responsibilities without explanation. He moved back to his home town in New York, secured a job, and never bothered to invite us to join him. During his absenteeism, I talked myself into believing I didn't need a dad, and that the abundant supply of love from my mom was enough. My anger regarding his absence was more on Kathy's behalf. His lack of interest in her life, emptiness of concern for her challenges, and cluelessness regarding her life details left me unable to soften my attitude toward him. I coiled when he expressed unwarranted anger toward Kathy as a sweet little girl. I don't remember him attending any of her childhood milestones. He never asked what her major was in college. I don't think he even spelled her name correctly. His abandonment of my sister was difficult for me to settle.

Only in later, more reflective times, would I understand my projection of defense. The six-year age difference between Kathy and I allowed a perspective for her that I didn't quite have for myself. Being fatherless was okay for me, but not for her. It would take years, but eventually I could see the role my mom played in their marital dysfunction. Until then, I was blinded by my allegiance to her—she carried the financial, emotional, and logistical burdens of single parenthood. My heart eventually softened for my dad. I came to understand he did the best he could do in life, but it wasn't nearly enough for his wife and children. His redemption came years later when he returned to care for my mom in her elderly years, allowing her to remain home where she wished to be. He also took his role as grandfather with far more intention than he ever did as father. His sideline attendance at all sporting events where grandkids participated was a given. I grew to appreciate my dad for his ability to give in ways he could. We all mellowed with time.

Although my mom had a troubled relationship with her adoptive mother, she adored her father. His occasional financial offerings, visits to Ohio, and unsolicited fatherly advice to my brothers left my mom glowing with love and admiration for him. He was larger than life in her eyes, and seemed to know when she needed a lifeline. One of the ways he helped was by taking the three of us on vacations, offering my mom opportunities to simply get away. I think my grandfather was astute enough to know the burdens she carried, and inviting us to join him on one of his many world travels left us all giddy. Packing for Caribbean cruises warranted frivolous shopping trips to second-hand clothing stores. We all needed a formal dress to wear to "Captain's Night," after all. Vacations with my grandfather were a treat, culminating with our grandest excursion of all: a trip to the British Isles.

I was 17 at the time, and Kathy was 11. We had never been overseas before, and the anticipated opportunity for my mom to visit the birthplace of her natural parents opened our experience of what family meant. Walking along the lush green lands, meeting people that shared her heritage, and wrapping herself in the cable-knit spirit of the mother and father she never knew were especially poignant. We rode a double-decker bus in London and kissed the Blarney Stone as my grandfather reveled in our laughter and joy. The trip was enchanting; that is, until he became ill.

The last leg of our trip landed us in Scotland. While touring a castle somewhere in the outskirts of Edinburgh, my grandfather stated he didn't feel well. He sat on a bench as my mom searched out a nearby coffee shop for some warm soup, waiting for the tour bus to return to our hotel. Initially, we thought he simply needed the opportunity to rest. Concern rising, we returned to Edinburgh in search of medical treatment. Within hours, he was admitted to an Edinburgh hospital and diagnosed with pneumonia. Two days later he died. The unexpected and tragic turn of events left us devastated.

The vacation tour moved on without us. My mom, Kathy, and I were left alone in this friendly but foreign country, lost amidst the shudder of our unexpected loss. Our first order of business was to arrange transfer of my grandfather's body to his home in New York City.

My mom didn't collapse into her deeply personal grief. Within the realm of shock, I recall her strength, self-control, and determination to do right by her father who'd served in World War I—by bringing him honorably home one last time. Arm in arm, we walked against the flow of clustered pedestrian traffic in the heart of the city; she held tight to Kathy and me. We navigated our way down this unfamiliar street, putting one foot in front of the other in search of the American Embassy. Step by step, we walked in sync. This new stride would define our dynamic as mother and daughters: this was the metaphor which pitted the three of us as one unifying force. Then, and forever after, my mom held on to what she knew was sure and steady and true: her daughters. This moment, too, cast the dye of sisterhood. We could walk any road before us as long as we did it together, arm in arm.

✢ chapter 3 ✢

As my sister and I grew older, married, and created families of our own, our bond intensified and our family lives meshed. Our children grew up together. We enjoyed random "toddy times," where late afternoon texts reading, "toddy?" meant within 10 minutes we were sitting together outside in the summer or huddled by the fireplace in the winter, sipping a glass of wine and catching up with random chatter. More times than not, Mark or Phil would show up with a loosened tie from work ready to join the sisters enjoying one another. Our kids flowed in and out of toddy times until they were old enough to join us, and then the circle expanded.

Gerry, Kathy, and I living in the same zip code meant we could share the responsibilities associated with our aging mom. As oldness and frailty overtook her, a need for us intensified. Years of smoking left her breathless and weak in physical stamina. Falls became more frequent. Hospitalizations, surgeries, and periods of inpatient rehabilitation left her especially dependent on more daughter intervention. Her world became smaller and isolation more evident. Her body endured a slow and tortuous breakdown. Once she lost her ability to drive, her relationship to the world beyond her dark and cluttered family room diminished. We knew she needed us, which meant we needed one another more.

Kathy and I talked daily, sometimes more than once, to navigate the continual challenge of caring for my mom. Sunday afternoons we powwowed, negotiating a schedule for the week ahead. We took turns arranging "outings" for our mom so as to maximize the opportunities for her to get out of the house. Despite our best efforts to meet her needs as well as preserve balance in our own lives, sometimes we needed to show up even when we didn't want to.

Many mornings I would sit at my kitchen table following the school routine of getting my kids out the door and on the bus. Warming my hands around the mug of freshly poured coffee, the phone rang predictably around 9 a.m. Honestly, I wanted nothing more than to ignore the persistent ring and let the answering machine solve my dilemma, but instead I answered with false enthusiasm.

"Hi Missy," my mom would say, calling me by my childhood nickname.

"Hi Mom, how're you doing this morning?" Kneading my forehead, already I knew my day was hijacked.

The routine was the same. My mom asked me what was new. She wondered what I had on tap for the day. There was a pause of longing in her voice, and then I'd say,

"Hey Mom, I have some errands to do today. Do you want to keep me company?" Her voice lifted, and every time she said yes.

"That would be so nice," she'd say.

Too fragile to go in and out of stores, my mom enjoyed the ride of the mundane. She remained in the car while I navigated a checklist of errands. I didn't really need toothpaste, but a quick trip to Walgreens topped my to-do list. Surely there were some blouses that needed to go to the dry cleaner. I wouldn't want to leave her too long in the car alone, so a grocery stop might include a quick grab of bread and a gallon of milk. I seemed to take the long route between stops allowing more time to do nothing together. Always, we went to Wendy's for a drive-thru lunch. My mom loved their Jr. Bacon Cheeseburger and an iced tea with extra ice and extra lemon. We sat in the parking lot as she relished the refreshment of the "really cold" iced tea and "hit-the-spot" sandwich.

Every time I was with my mom, it was like catching a glimpse to a hummingbird's wings fluttering alongside a blooming flower. Stilled by the allurement of wonder, my mom had a way of pulling you into the marvel of the commonplace. Sitting in the passenger seat, she came alive with joy. Each outing connected her with the beauty of the ordinary. Something was always accessible to her.

"I don't think the colors of the trees have ever been more beautiful," she said every October.

"I do love to see the snowflakes fall," she whispered almost to herself as we navigated winter wonderlands. "Did you know no two snowflakes are alike?" she added, struck by the awe and beauty just beyond her windowpane.

"The grass is growing so quickly! Look at those blooming daffodils?" she said with glee as we discovered the new growth of spring.

And my favorite...

"Just look at those clouds," she admired. Her gaze lingered upward. There, floating in the blue sky were the cloud images of a dog, a flower, a lamb, or whatever else her aging eyes created. She reached over from her passenger seat, grasped my arm and said with delight and gratitude, "Oh, thank you Missy! I really needed this. Today's just been wonderful."

I admit quite honestly that my heart was often ungenerous upon hearing the phone on those unscheduled mornings.

Invariably, I called Kathy on my way to pick up my mom. Anyone else could have misunderstood the self-centered complaint, but the need to say my reluctance out loud fell on safe ears. Kathy understood because predictably tomorrow would be her day. We reminded one another of the importance of our daughter-works. Our mom, after all, was our greatest mentor in how to love. And despite our grumbles, she never failed to uplift. When I returned her home, safely back to her rose-colored velveteen armchair, her good-bye embrace told me how much she appreciated getting out.

After each one of these outings, I was eager to talk with Kathy. Without explanation, my sister understood my mom's ability to transform selfish inconvenience to humility and re-acquaintance with the treasure of her. Every time, my mom reminded me of the extraordinary in the ordinary and the delight in the simplest of pleasures; her joy in simply being with us imprinted our hearts. And every time, Kathy and I lifted one another in support, understanding, and reminders of how blessed we were to have our mom as our mom.

☙ chapter 4 ☙

March 17, 2013

Kathy and Phil's oldest child, Bridget, was in her final year at Xavier University in Cincinnati. The news of her brother's accident left her, too, in a state of encroaching panic. Bridget, Jack, and I left early the morning after Conor's injury and spent the 4½-hour drive praying and preparing ourselves for what would greet us on arrival. I tried to center myself, knowing each Crippen would need a different part of me. Bridget's capacity to love was fierce, especially when it came to her brothers. While driving, she reminisced about recent conversations with Conor. Each recollection added to the disbelief of his accident. *How could this be happening?*

Jack sat in the back seat, quiet. Unlike his sister whose transparency left little doubt regarding her emotional state, Jack internalized his torment. His worry settled in the deep places of his gut where reason didn't exist. Without logic, Jack took responsibility for his brother's accident. If only he'd answered Conor's phone call the previous night during pre-dance photos, if only he'd returned the call, if only…if only…then Conor wouldn't have been hit by the car. Despair makes us think crazy sometimes. It would take Jack a while to work through this skewed thinking.

Common experiences within the confines of family may seem

25

inconsequential, but the culmination of everyday coexistence yields relationship treasures. When an older brother teaches a younger sister how to ride a bike, or when arguments surface after hogging a bathroom, or when shared kitchen duties are assigned by a weekly schedule magnetized to the refrigerator door, the sweetness of lifelong bonds is bred. Kathy and Phil nurtured the concept of family and maintained their learned philosophy from my mom that siblings were one another's greatest gifts. Bridget, Conor, and Jack were a unit; a trio that only worked because they had each other. Three is what they'd always known. Without Conor, the other two were lost.

We walked into the hospital lobby, searching for Kathy and Phil. The drive from Dayton, Ohio to Chicago provided time to prepare for what I intuitively knew would expand all limits of sisterhood. I tried to shake the chill of the Chicago winter as I searched for my sister among the swarm of people lingering around the reception desk. It was late on a Sunday morning. The hospital lobby was calm, typical for a weekend morning. We found Kathy and Phil by the elevator. She embraced Bridget and Jack, caressing their faces in reassurance. I saw her willing demeanor; telling them amidst uncertainty it would be okay. I stayed back, allowing them to reset themselves in their new family reality.

I waited and then saw Kathy walk toward me. I saw the uncertainty of Conor's condition threaten her deceivingly steady gait. I enveloped her in my arms. I felt it all. I felt her world, now turned upside-down. I felt her fear, her concern, and her unknowing. I felt her passionate love for Conor as she whispered in my ear, "Just give me the road. I don't care how long it takes, just give me the road." I felt her need for me as she returned to her family, preparing Bridget and Jack for Conor's appearance.

Huddled as a unit, the Crippens entered the elevator. I stayed behind, hoping somehow Kathy could still feel the power of my embrace. I turned from the elevator, not sure where to go.

⚡ chapter 5 ⚡

Quiet and often to himself, for some reason my brother Pat and I didn't cultivate any kind of unique sibling stamp. We missed the opportunity to share that distinctive connection that brothers and sisters experience. I'm not sure why we never uniquely connected. To this day, my lack of personal memories with my oldest brother leaves me with an unsettled grief.

Kathy, on the other hand, shared deep and mutual affection with Pat, epitomizing the best kind of big brother/little sister bond. When Kathy was a baby, Pat used to lie on the floor next to her rocking the infant bassinette until she fell asleep. His patience with her had no limit and his desire to protect her was fierce. Their 13-year age gap facilitated that kind of sibling tenderness, free from antagonism or rivalry. Pat stepped into the role of father as my dad's emotional absence created a vacuum of paternal affection. Kathy, so innocent and safe, offered an unconditional love my brother's broken soul so desperately needed: she muted the demons gaining speed in his fight for life. The tenderness between them complemented one another. Their bond was well recognized.

While in college, Pat called Kathy often, wanting to check and make sure she was okay. He sent her birthday cards with signatures from all the other guys on his dorm floor. Pat spent a good part of his wedding reception walking the parking lot with a tearful nine-year-old little sister, reassuring her that getting married did not mean he was abandoning her. He hated to see her in pain, and her tears broke his heart.

The onset of Pat's journey with mental illness hit us hard. One early September night, and for reasons that still remain a mystery, at the age of 16, my brother sat on the bathroom floor and drank Drano drain cleaner. The caustic acid totally corroded the lining of his esophagus and landed him in the intensive care unit in critical condition. The damage was life-threatening and would leave him compromised in ability to swallow or eat with ease for the remainder of his life. We never knew why he would do such a random and destructive thing. I'm not sure if anyone ever really asked him. We were shrouded in those days by denial, avoidance, and silence. Was this a suicide attempt? Was he having problems in high school, was he being bullied, or did Pat have a limited ability to absorb our parents' dysfunction? We just didn't know, and to my knowledge, we didn't talk about it. The regret of not understanding or reaching into his pain would haunt us forever. I'll always be sorry I wasn't more aware, tell him I loved him, or sit with him as he drank the calorie-jacked eggnog shakes my mom made him several times a day post-surgery.

Diagnosed with bipolar disorder in his early 20's, Pat struggled. Although he was challenged with the balance of medications and episodes of emotional breakdown, that didn't define him. Pat loved to laugh, and he loved fun. He was smart, sensitive, caring, and could assemble a 2000-piece puzzle in the blink of an eye. Although personal demons fought for mind space, his fun-loving essence surprised us sometimes. Take, for example, the time he insisted we stalk Kathy and Phil on their first date.

The rule in our house was you weren't allowed to date until the age of 16. Only a sophomore in high school and not quite 16, my sister was asked to go to dinner by a senior, stretching the boundaries of acceptable "first date" criteria. It was a good thing my mom was impressed by this redhead named Phil Crippen because she gave Kathy permission to go. That didn't preclude us from having some fun at the expense of the "baby" of the family. Much to my sister's embarrassment, my mom, Pat, Gerry, Mark, and I went to the restaurant of their first date. We huddled together, hiding behind the fake fern trees in the bar where we spied, not so stealthily. Laughter gave us away, and Phil ended up joining us, which was probably why my mom agreed for them to have a second date. It was Pat's approval of Phil, however, that gave Kathy permission of the heart. The seeds of young love were planted.

Pat could never really settle into ease, and despite his profound love for his young son, Michael, the internal voices of sadness and despair blared louder than the sweeter songs of life. Eventually, his despair got the best of him. On November 7, 1984, at the age of 30, he drove to the eastern shore of Texas, sat on the beach in his car and shot himself in the chest.

I was newly married at the time and received an early morning call from Gerry. It was a Tuesday, and I was about ready to leave for work. We knew Pat had been missing for two days, but never could have imagined such a tragic and violent end. How could he ever have justified leaving us and, more importantly, leaving Michael? It was so confusing, so shocking, and so deeply sad. My mom asked me to drive to Kathy's school and tell her. Neil and Gerry were scrambling to find flights to Texas in order to bring our brother home, and I suspect my mom was immobilized by her devastation. I am quite certain she was paralyzed by the

Anne Marie Romer

images of excruciating anguish. *How could this be?*

Mark and I drove to our alma mater, Archbishop Alter High School in Kettering, Ohio, and went to the Main Office. We were greeted by the office secretaries with an embrace. The close-knit Catholic high school maintained community bonds long after students graduated. Teachers and administrators knew my brothers, they knew Mark and I, and they knew my sister, then a senior. The principal, once Mark's algebra teacher, met us with her signature bear hug, then looked at us with knitted eyebrows. She inquired why we were there, reading the mist in our eyes. I told her Pat had died, and that we needed to see Kathy. She pulled me into her arms and embraced me. It was as if she armed me with the stuff of strength, propelling me with heart muscle that I would in turn need to give my sister.

How do you even find words like "he's dead," or "he shot himself," and then have to repeat them over again because Kathy couldn't grasp the fact that Pat was gone? As we sat in the principal's office, I felt her abandonment and bewildered sorrow. I knew how much she adored Pat for so many reasons. He stepped into the shoes of the father who was never present. Now he, too, had also left her on purpose. I held my sister as she sobbed; this 17-year-old who already had suffered too much loss. I couldn't cry. All my tears I gave to her.

Life stopped as we tried to manage confusion, loss, and the violent means of Pat's passing. Bewilderment laced our sorrow. No matter how much we tried to understand, Pat was gone.

Time between death and ceremonial "closure" offers the opportunity to exist within a cocoon where being together provides a safety net for grieving. We did as a family what would become much more familiar over the years. We gathered, sat around the dining room table, and remained encased in the cloak of support that we, as a whole, could offer one another. And of course, sure enough, we laughed our way through the shock of Pat's passing. We remembered the way he told his one signature joke, The Wide Mouth Frog. We shared the visual of how he giggled with his entire body when Neil made him laugh. We looked in one another's eyes for the twinkle so often seen in Pat's look when he was immersed in family delight. We tried to replicate his voice as shared stories highlighted him in the best of times. We solidified our brand of coping. Together we navigated the unthinkable.

Pat's self-inflicted death meant that as a family, we could never be whole again. Pat was not only the oldest, he was the smartest, the gentlest, and the most beautiful of our sibling unit. Now we were four siblings, and the model of how to exist had to be redesigned. Pat's death heightened our awareness of family worth. We became more intentional with one another. We opened up and talked more. We sought more opportunities to be together. The importance of family became our mantra. Under the constant direction of our mom, we promised to be more attentive; vowing never to let another become lost in the abyss of anguish. *Never again* we repeated. For the next 30 years, we reaffirmed our commitment. We pledged to have no more regret, and we honored Pat by being more intentional with our love and support. *Never again.* Over time, life resumed a new normal with Pat as our champion for hope. So, when the despondent story repeated itself 30 years later, we were stunned.

chapter 6

Chicago

Gerry arrived at Advocate Illinois Masonic Hospital in Chicago shortly after I did. Our eyes bored into one another, connecting our inability to find words of disbelief that this was really happening. Walking into the SICU offered no option to spool back to yesterday. Just 24 hours prior, Conor was thriving, learning, and living the care-free life of a college student. In an instant, the course of his life was altered. Replacing the task of studying for midterms was the fight for mere survival.

· · · · ·

A note regarding the driver of the car that hit Conor. The truth is, I really don't know much about him. I know he was intoxicated, and his car was speeding well over the limit. I'm certain my sister knows more about him, but the fact is both she and Phil chose from the very beginning to keep their gaze forward. I don't even know his name. The Crippens worked through the legal aftermath of the driver's recklessness, but neither of them talked much about that piece of the story. They would not allow themselves or anyone else surrounding Conor to be distracted by anger, resentment, or calls for restitution. The fight for Conor's life was their focus. For months, I would hear the question from well-meaning people, "What happened to the driver?" My honest answer was and is still the same: I really don't know. That piece to this story will remain powerless in moving forward to tell this remarkable healing journey and search for the kind of energy which breeds life.

. . . . .

Conor was manicured in the hospital bed, his face obstructed by ventilator tubes, probes, and wires working in tandem to keep him alive. Given the ferocious 30-foot trajectory of his fall, his head gave no indication of the trauma endured, and other than some bruising around his eyes, he looked eerily perfect beneath the cloak of medical equipment competing for space. We were not being fooled by the angelic look on his face or his sleepy demeanor, however. The hiss of the life-supporting ventilator brought a rise and fall to his chest, a humble reminder of his fragile state. A neck brace kept his head immobilized. A bolt was placed through his skull to measure the increasing pressure on his brain. A central intravenous line was taped to the side of his chest. His legs were encased in air compressors to maintain adequate circulation. Medications from multiple automated pumps infused sedatives, antibiotics, and fluid nutrition into his blood. Pillows flanked his arms and legs, creating alignment to minimize skin breakdown. A color-coded monitor was attached to the console pole system, providing real-time indicators of his condition. In his medically induced coma, blood pressure, heart rhythms, temperature, oxygen levels, and the increasingly important intracranial pressure (ICP) gauged the immediate aftermath of his brain trauma. Yet, despite the growing evidence that his injury was serious, we felt the energy of Conor's spirit thrive. Not only that, we were keenly aware this could have been much worse. There were no broken bones except for the trauma to his skull and head. There were no other internal injuries. His legs were intact; his feet still had the high arch that enabled him to run like a gazelle. The fact that significant injury was limited to brain trauma was indeed something to be grateful for. This was our initial orientation to resting in the marvel. From the outset, we surrendered to the awe of goodness.

Kathy slipped her hand beneath his, hoping he would recognize her touch. Still wearing her slippers from home, my sister took vigil at Conor's side. She later reflected, "I saw my son. I saw my champion of adversity and my guy who owned my heart. I saw his hand and was so happy to hold it. I kissed and kissed and whispered and touched all that I could." She willed him with the history of their relationship. While he was growing up, breakfast conversations between Kathy and Conor revolved around the whys and hows of life. Even at a young age, Conor sought to stretch his mind, opening himself to possibilities that could bring forth purpose. Meld that kind of intensity with a mischievous desire to create fun and frivolity, and you have a young man that embodies leadership, magnetism, and infectious charm. This unwelcome detour of life was stunning and catastrophic; yet in an odd way, the fact that he looked so beautiful and peaceful…maybe was a sign that all would be well. Kathy's constructive approach and choice to believe Conor's accident could be part of a larger, more meaningful context was the only way she could cope as she caressed the fingers of her son so broken from another's carelessness. Maybe this was the pathway by which Conor could realize his full potential. As the doctors tried to explain "traumatic brain injury," Kathy held on to optimism.

Phil, on the other hand, was terrified. The reality of Conor's grave condition was evident to him. Sugar-coating the critical state of his son with belief that what lay before him was some kind of destiny couldn't penetrate his fear.

The Glasgow Coma Scale is used by emergency personnel to assess brain injury. The GCS provides valuation based on three criteria: a person's ability to open eyes and the levels of verbal and motor responses. The evaluation range is between 3 and 15. A minimum score of 3 has the worst prognosis, and a score of 8 has potential for good recovery. A "normal" person who can open eyes on command, is oriented and can obey motor direction, would probably yield a GCS score of 15. Once a brain is injured, the score can significantly change, decreasing with a patient's inability to respond. Patients with a score between 3 and 8 are usually considered to be comatose; an assessment under 5 is potentially fatal.[1] Conor presented to the Emergency Department with a Glasgow Coma Score of 3. Not only was he unresponsive, his condition offered slim hope for survival.

Dr. Juan Santiago-Gonzalez was the trauma physician on call that night. A Code Yellow announcement preceded Conor's arrival, alerting staff that a trauma patient was being transferred by squad. Later we would learn that just days prior to his accident, Conor met Dr. Santiago while volunteering at the Illinois Masonic Hospital. Dr. Santiago told my sister he recognized Conor that night as he worked tirelessly to improve his status to a GCS of 5 still within serious and concerning parameters. When my sister had the chance to meet Dr. Santiago, she went to hug him in appreciation for his efforts. He stopped her, indicating Conor's situation was fragile and tenuous. Instead of hugging, he suggested she pray, and pray hard. The clinicians knew it would get worse before any possibility of improvement. The fact was Conor's condition was grave, and he was hanging on to a thread

[1] "Glasgow Coma Scale—CDC Mass Trauma Preparedness." *Centers for Disease Control and Prevention*, Centers for Disease Control and Prevention, www.cdc.gov/masstrauma/resources/gcscale.htm.

for life. Still, we were clueless to the scope of potential brain damage that was still yet to be determined.

What we didn't understand at the time was that the initial head injury, although critical, was just the beginning. For the next week, we watched Conor's cranial pressure increase, and then increase some more. Trauma to any part of the body can cause swelling, and swollen tissue needs space to expand. Because the brain is encased within the confines of a bony skull, there is little room for the traumatized soft brain tissue to expand. Dr. Sean McCarney, one of the surgical residents offered reassurance to Kathy and Phil, explained the danger of a secondary injury with regard to brain trauma. Once areas like the brain stem are starved of much-needed blood circulation, their functions begin to shut down, threatening the ability to thrive. Days following the accident, Conor's inability to breathe on his own, a rising body temperature, and increased blood pressure indicated his brain injury was still active. In other words, the Crippens were settling in for a wild ride through uncharted terrain. Their son was very, very sick.

As I tried to comprehend this unfathomable scene in the intensive care unit, a memory with my mom came to haunt me. Weeks before she died, I was sitting with her while she ate dinner. By then, Gerry, Kathy, and I shared the responsibilities of bringing my parents meals each day, and then we would put my mom to bed. Hospice outpatient care was involved, and we all knew the end of life was nearing. Sharing the last meal of her day gave us the opportunity to talk about whatever was on her mind or in her heart as she contemplated death.

One such evening, my mom tried to work her way through leftover Chicken Divan or some other casserole that was my yesterday's dinner. Her appetite waned, and even the effort to chew her food was taxing on her weakened state. Her chair armrests were worn and soiled from her last years of sedentary life. The hiss of her oxygen tank was constant. Her body was tired. I could tell by the translucent thinning of her bruised skin and her fatigue in even trying to breathe. She took my hand; the strength of her grip defied the fact that her body was fading.

"I worry about your sister," she said. I was taken aback.

"What do you mean, Mom? Why do you worry?" I asked, perplexed. Was she concerned about how my sister would cope after her passing? Was she worried about Kathy's tenacity or emotional strength? Sure, Kathy's capacity to feel deeply could be mistaken for vulnerability, but my mom and I knew Kathy was anything but weak. I was puzzled by her concern. I didn't ask for further clarification. Reflecting now, I wish I had.

I encircled her hand with both of mine.

"Mom," I said, "you don't need to worry about Kath. She has Phil and she has me. We'll always take care of her."

The week preceding my mom's death, our family had the unique opportunity to say goodbye. As we kept vigil at her bedside, she reassured us that she would never leave us, and that she would continue to care for all of us from the heavens.

"My love will always find you," she said, pointing her finger toward the ceiling in determination.

As I sat beside my sister at Advocate Illinois Masonic observing her rise in strength, I thought about what my mom said to me. I wondered if, in that holding pattern between life and death, she somehow knew Kathy would be thrust into this shattered world. Until now, Kathy and I shared all of life, all triumphs, all heartaches, and every call to action in caring for our mom. We grieved together after loss, and along with Gerry, shared an impenetrable sibling bond.

This time, Kathy was on her own. And although my mission was to remain by her side, I couldn't arrange a schedule to share the burden. I couldn't pow-wow with her on a Sunday afternoon and plan the week ahead in partnership. This was hers. I knew what my mom meant when she expressed worry about Kathy, and I could only hope her spirit could reach my sister somehow.

News of Conor's accident spread through the Dayton and Loyola communities like wildfire, fueled by the immediacy of social media. I was sitting with Bridget the day after arrival to Chicago as the Crippen cell phones were igniting with emails and texts inquiring about Conor's condition. Facebook was an unfamiliar entity to me at the time, but Bridget and I recognized quickly the need to control the information and rumors regarding the accident and Conor's condition. Bridget and I, through her tutorial, created a Facebook page, "Prayer Request for Conor" (PRFC), designed to provide Conor's supporters up-to-date information regarding his condition as well as a vehicle for prayerful intention for his healing. In two days' time, we were reaching thousands of people, yielding a platform for conversation between the Crippens and a multitude of others who came to know Conor's story. Soon, it felt like a movement. Just two days following his accident I wrote an entry on Conor's Facebook page. Many more followed.

March 19, 2013, PRFC

Conor had a relatively quiet night. The pressure in his brain elevated again, however, and is being given medication to keep that lowered. The silver lining, however, is that he is more responsive to intervention and is initiating coughing on his own. There are more limb movements especially on the right side. My sister's take is that Conor (never known to be particularly patient when achieving goals) is readying himself to wake up. He is initiating respirations more, and he is just plain looking better. His CT scan from this morning was OK, and the docs feel comfortable enough not doing a daily scan providing he remains stable. We are settling in for another quiet day as more rest is what he still needs.

I cannot tell you how lifted we feel by your continued prayers. The flow of bold intention for him is working. My sister and I were talking about how this feels like a true perfect storm of all that God provides. Conor, with his unique and determined essence, the thorough and loving care by his medical team, and the presence of God through each and every one of you leaves us without doubt that our adored and cherished Conor is working his way to wholeness.

Tonight, in the hospital chapel, Conor's friends joined us for a rosary prayer. Witnessing these young kids pull rosary beads out of their pockets was a reflection of their commitment in prayer for Conor. We prayed for hope, faith, movement of the Spirit, intercession by all the heavenly angels who are so strongly vested in him, and vigilance for ALL of us as we move through these tough but hopeful days. Kathy, Phil and the rest of us are profoundly thankful to all of you. We hear you and ask that you remain vigilant with us.

I ask you all to remain with us as we collectively pray Conor's way to recovery. Believe me, someday very soon when Bridget and Jack read to him all of your prayers, he will not only be humbled and grateful, but in true Conor form, he will return to the world all he has been given in hope and faith.

We move on to tomorrow with hope. We are so grateful to all of you. Please continue to pray.

Once Conor was admitted to the SICU, his physicians and nurses commanded his critical condition with poise, confidence, and competence. His condition was erratic, requiring constant monitoring. Brain trauma plays havoc with basic life functions like heart rate, breathing capabilities, and the body's ability to regulate itself. The nurses and physicians evaluated minute to minute, trying to remain in control of his wavering condition. Things could be stable one minute, and the next could be beeping indicators that he needed urgent intervention.

Kathy's instinct was to speak to her son: caress his brow, and reassure him with her tender touch and hopeful words. The medical counsel, however, was to remain quiet and non-interactive with him. The less stimulation the better, in an attempt to minimize brain activity and control further swelling. This defied the conventional and maternal wisdom on how to care for a sick child. The directive to essentially leave him alone was frustrating. Still, she remained by his side and gently entwined their fingers, repeating her constant but silent prayers.

From the outset, my sister had a curious reaction to Conor's accident. Providing comfort, even in the dark hours of intense worry, was her lack of surprise that this happened. Bridget, upon hearing of Conor's accident, had a fleeting moment when she knew in some way this was Conor's fate. Like Bridget, Kathy had an intuition that Conor would be challenged in this way. Although she could have never imagined his path to changing the world would come in the form of a brain injury, her trust in Conor's spiritual purpose gave wind beneath the wings of her tenacity. The possibility of Conor being defined by the tragedy of his accident did not exist in her mind. Rather, it would be a significant chapter in a bigger story of triumph. Since Conor's early childhood, my sister's mission was to nurture her son so that he could realize fully his God-given purpose. The accident illuminated an unexpected path, but Kathy never flinched in her interpretation of the event: Conor, despite lying comatose in critical condition, was just getting started.

Bridget and I spent the first days in the SICU as backup team. When Kathy and Phil needed a shower break or opportunity to rest their weary minds, Bridget and I would take over, sitting with Conor, hoping he could sense our family community of healing love. We felt as if our tight relationship took on new meaning as we remained in the dark, quiet room next to him. My orientation into Bridget's life from the day of her birth included Godmother, second mother, gene pool comrade with blue eyes, and all-around supporter-in-chief. Although we were able to find snippets of levity as we sat by her brother, one afternoon Bridget was overwhelmed by the scene before her. She took Conor's hand, laid her head on the bed and began to sob. The fatigue and disbelief over the past days unleashed. I rubbed her quivering back and brushed the hair from her moistened cheeks. Yes, I tried to comfort her, but then I reminded her of the possibility that Conor might sense her emotional angst. I gently suggested she take a deep breath, and then advised her again. As her sniffles continued, I used that second-mother voice, albeit a whisper.

"Bridget, do you need to step outside?"

She looked at me, laughed, and wiped away the rest of her tears, saving them for another time. Our relationship grew even deeper as we sat together. As she collected herself above the temptation to collapse into despair, I saw my young niece rise up to become a brighter beacon—not only for Conor, but for the rest of her family as well. Her vigil would not include words of goodbye. Rather, we all needed to lock arms in belief that our Conor could survive and embrace this second chance at abundant life.

Bridget's life mission was being redirected right before my eyes. Courage replaced anxiety, and the sustained pledge to remain in trust replaced carefree college life. Bridget, too, was rising up.

Kathy committed to remain with Conor for as long as he needed to be in Chicago. None of us knew how long that would be, but the advice from one of the SICU physicians to "forward your mail" indicated that the return trip home would not be anytime soon. Kathy took a leave of absence from her elementary teaching position with Stingley Elementary School in Centerville, a suburb of Dayton so she could remain by Conor's side. Phil, on the other hand, needed to make sure everything else in their world continued to turn. He would commute from home to Chicago, sometimes several times a week, to fulfill his work obligations and make sure Jack had some sort of normalcy while attending to his studies. As resignation to the fact that Conor's hospitalization would last at least weeks, Phil and I created an arrangement so that Kathy would never be alone in Chicago. I committed to be with my sister when Phil could not. Commuting north on I-65 in Indiana included phone conversations with Phil as he updated me on Conor's condition and Kathy's state of mind. Sitting beside her, pleading silently to the heavens, was the only thing I could do.

∗ chapter 7 ∗

My mom died in February 2012. Neil, Gerry, Kathy, and I remained in close contact as we tried to adjust to life without the encouragement of her love. Recollections of her delight when we were together charged us to remain even more connected. Her mission, cultivated from her own craving, was for us to be close. *Always take care of each another.* Her words ricocheted between us like the echo from a mountain top. Her longing for a brother or a sister never tolerated lingering discord in her children. *Always remember how lucky you are to have each other.* Neil, true to his loyal allegiance to family, suggested we gather on St. Patrick's Day at the local Irish pub. It had been five weeks since our mom's death. We needed to be together.

Michael, Pat's son, now married with children, came from Lexington. Neil drove from Nashville. Photographs of us wearing green, celebrating our Irish heritage, reflected the joy of being reunited. Along with Phil and Mark, we felt our new version of wholeness despite the vast void of our mom. Michael made tangible Pat's connection. I was reminded of how reassuring touch can be. The ability to hug or slip my arm safely into the crooks of my siblings' arms were reminders of the surety that shared lineage offers. I felt comfort as we spent the day together.

It wasn't until the day turned toward dusk that the mood changed. As the brightness of the day faded, so did the glow in

Neil's eyes. I read his aura, and the deeper I paid attention to his look, the more sadness I sensed. I challenged him by asking, "Are you okay?" I pressed his flat "I'm fine," as I was quite familiar with the façade and guise he could fashion so well. My mom could see through him, but she was now gone. It was up to us to make an attempt to open him up. We knew his recent divorce left him brokenhearted, and a failed business endeavor resulted in financial strain. The loss of our Mom seemed to leave him aimlessness in matters of the heart, perhaps even more than the rest of us knew.

My well-meaning interrogation in the crowded bar was cluttered by noise and pitchers of green beer being passed overhead. I summoned our family unit to step outside so that we could once and for all pressure Neil into telling us what was wrong. My intuition screamed a warning.

"Lung cancer," he said, followed by, "**terminal** lung cancer."

We stood in silence, stunned. *Wait, what did you say?* We were paralyzed with disbelief.

And then we barraged him with questions. "How do you know this? What tests have you done? Who's your doctor? What do you mean, 'terminal?' What about treatment?"

We held him, trying to reassure him with our resolve. Neil went on to say he would not agree to treatment, to which our response was confusion and disbelief. My husband Mark, an oncologist who spent his professional life treating cancer patients, asked questions to which Neil had no answers. He couldn't relay any specifics. Without information regarding a pathology report, diagnostic testing, or physician names, the situation seemed curious. Why couldn't he tell us more? I thought it was strange, but I also acknowledged how shock can wipe any ability to recall. Many people have a tough time remembering anything after hearing "cancer," so Neil's inability to give us a more thorough report only meant we needed to intervene more. We weren't going to allow him to navigate this alone.

We came up with a frantic plan. We told him we would help him fight, that we could not accept his choice to give up. Sensing Neil's resignation, we rallied around him with a mobilizing energy. Kathy reminded him of our commitment to one another. Michael's presence alone was a plea. The possibility of losing Neil threatened to rip open the old wounds for Michael, who had suffered from too much loss already.

We remained with one another in the twilight of this warm St. Patrick's Day, trying to craft a collective response to this bombshell. Little did I know those vibrations I so keenly felt shaking my insides would soon be a monumental quake.

Following St. Patrick's Day, worry hijacked our every thought, but still, something felt off. Neil had lost weight and his face appeared sunken and gray, as if disease took residence in his body. His 30-year smoking habit did leave him with a higher risk of lung disease. I was trying to validate this surreal announcement with some backdrop of evidence, but there was still a huge disconnect of factual support.

Neil returned to Nashville with a promise that he would ask his old and dear friend, Dave Carney, to go with him to the medical appointments the following week scheduled at the Vanderbilt University Medical Center. Neil and Dave had been friends since high school, and Dave's willingness to accompany Neil to doctor's visits or diagnostic testing gave us peace of mind. Dave's wife Pam was an oncology nurse at Vanderbilt, so we felt Neil was in good hands for this round of information gathering. They both genuinely loved Neil, and reassured us they would be his eyes and ears over the next few days.

Gerry, Kathy, and I sensed a deep sadness in Neil which was perplexing. Already he seemed resigned to hopelessness. He talked of dying. His proclamation of love for us and requests to look after his daughter Megan yielded unease. He told us of the Cat Stevens song he wanted played at his funeral. How could he be giving up before the journey even started? Where was his fight? Where was his accountability to life? Something wasn't adding up. I reassured Neil that the journey before him was about healing, as I knew my brother was in need of intense mending in both body and spirit.

I prayed. I prayed to my mom and Pat. I prayed through my disbelief and shock. My mom's ashes were in a simple wooden box on a bookshelf in my den awaiting the time when Neil, Gerry, Kathy, and I would spread them together in a nearby nature reserve encased by a canopy of trees. I could only imagine the occasion it would have been. The four of us would have laughed, cried, been a bit irreverent, and undoubtedly made the final expression of love an occasion to remember. The ashes took a back seat as I circumvented the grief of my mom's passing and desperately prayed for Neil.

The days following his announcement were long and anxious. The Wednesday following our St. Patrick's Day gathering was to include the CT Scan. I left that Tuesday for a long-planned trip to Florida with Mark and our daughters. I was reluctant to leave home, but knew it would take several days for bloodwork and test results, as well as recommendations for treatment. By that time, I'd be back and available. That morning I called Neil to tell him I was praying so hard, that I loved him so much, and to reiterate my hope. He didn't answer.

That Wednesday was a beautiful day in Florida. We enjoyed the sun and warmth, but I was more than a bit preoccupied. I frequently checked my phone. The early morning progressed with no word from Neil. As afternoon approached, I checked Mark's cell phone and saw a message from a 615-area code: Nashville. The message was from Dave Carney.

"Something's seriously wrong," Dave said. His recorded voice bled concern. Dave went on to say Neil didn't go to his scheduled test that day and he was actually driving back to Dayton. He instructed us to call immediately.

I felt the situation ramp up in chaos and frantic mystery. Mark and I called Dave. I desperately needed clarity, but not the kind I received.

"Last night Neil tried to kill himself," Dave said. I asked him to repeat what he'd just said as I was sure I heard wrong. I was in absolute disbelief. My insides began to quiver, and I knew there was no lung cancer. It was all a sham of desperation.

I immediately called Gerry and Kathy to inform them of what I learned, which was sketchy in detail. They, too, were speechless with shock. What we knew for sure was that Neil was on his way home. Gerry and Kathy agreed to be together when he arrived in Dayton. I heard muster in their voices. They would welcome our brother and embrace whatever brokenness he brought with him. I felt a collective compassion flow between us; we were ready to surround Neil with love and support in a way we never had with Pat—who didn't give himself or us a second chance at hope. Maybe we could enfold Neil towards wellness. My prayer was clear: *Just come home, Neil. Just come home.*

~ chapter 8 ~

Chicago

It was important for my sister to have each of Conor's caregivers know him: his essence pre-accident, and most importantly, the will and strength he embodied. Kathy became his voice. She spoke of his amazing spirit, engaging personality, sense of humor, and pointed ambition. His dreams included medical school, she would tell them. He wanted to be a neurologist, and was fascinated with the workings of the brain and the complexities of the mind, she added. Kathy talked of Conor as they repositioned his body and administered life-saving medications, and responded to alarming monitors with Conor-centered stories. She spent her days witnessing the attentive expertise of this SICU team, and had no choice but to release control and place utmost trust in the medical staff. Humility and helplessness left her in profound gratitude for each professional who ministered to Conor. These devoted SICU employees quickly became like family.

Make no mistake: the personal connections between patient, family, and medical staff instilled an awareness that Conor would not be going home anytime soon. His condition was acute. A cocktail of medications was tweaked to address his fluctuating condition. During these initial days post-accident, a drug-induced coma was indicated, as the severity to his brain's reaction to the injury was yet to be determined. Cooling blankets were applied when he spiked fevers. Ventilator settings were monitored to maximize the effects of mechanical breathing. Lung secretions were suctioned. Blood was drawn several times a day to monitor kidney function and the threat of infection. Conor was repositioned every two hours to prevent skin breakdown and the hospital team reacted medically to increased cranial pressures that required continual attention. Our world narrowed, defined by lab values, CT results, and color-coded monitor readings that oscillated far too often out of our comfort zone. The attention to his care was constant.

In these early days and weeks, we had no idea that nothing would be the same. We had no idea of what traumatic brain injury meant. We had no idea that every part of Conor would be wiped away like the sweep of an eraser on a chalkboard. We had no idea he would need to relearn, rebuild, and restore every capacity for independent function and thought. TBI returned him to a state of infancy. Everything was lost: his walk, his desires, his infectious laugh, his quest for learning, and his brilliant smile. His brain's ability to communicate was wiped away, as if access to the power grid for mind function was severed.

We didn't understand this yet. We were just hoping the brain would stop swelling and Conor would wake up. Then we could have him back. It seemed so simple.

The week following Conor's accident, Kathy and Phil kept vigil at Conor's bedside while episodes of ICP elevation caused increasing concern with the medical team. Dr. Kenji Muro, the neurosurgeon on call the night Conor presented to Masonic, made numerous visits to Conor's bedside each day with orders to adjust medications in hopes Conor's cranial pressure would stabilize. He noted one day that crafting a treatment plan for Conor was like solving a Rubik's Cube. I remember Dr. Muro saying that Conor suffered one of the most severe brain injuries he had seen in his professional career. By days three and four post-accident, his ICP levels reached into the 40's, causing grave concern with the medical team. Remember, normal brain pressure values range between 5 and 15.[2] Sustaining such high stress could only mean additional damage to vital areas of the brain, making any opportunity for recovery even more dim.

We sat and watched the critical numbers oscillate. The nurses adjusted sedative medications to deepen his coma, hoping to stop cranial pressure from increasing. Monitor alarms sounded when it wasn't working. We watched the numbers creep one minute, and then skyrocket in an instant. All we could do was rest in the belief that Conor's brain would calm. Kathy remained stalwart in her belief that Conor would navigate this grave time, but still she was helpless. I felt her call up bravery she never knew she embodied, from the depths of a soul she'd never tapped. I watched her pray. Her fingers worked the continual rosary chain. Sometimes I would hear the sniffle of her muffled cry. During these times, we sat together usually in silence. I remained in disbelief that Conor was so gravely ill, and that my sister's world now revolved around the color-coded monitor by his side.

Conor's accident defied all we thought we ever learned in life, as if God only dealt so many losing hands at the poker table. We used to believe there was some heavenly accountant who kept track of misfortunes bestowed on any one family. Fairness, after all, was only fair.

After a particularly volatile night, Kathy and Phil took turns in the recliner chair next to Conor, willing his brain swelling to quiet. I entered the SICU room in the morning to find my

---

[2] See TRAUMA.org website for information regarding intracranial pressure following trauma.

sister looking worn. Her sweatpants and long-sleeved fleece shirt looked crumpled from the night's vigil. Her face was pale, her hair tussled from the dark hours of restless disquiet. Phil looked no better.

Enough already! I silently cried to the heavens as I embraced my sister in plaintive prayer. How could this possibly be happening? Kathy's ability to carry burdens of the heart was exhausted. And then this: the senseless threat to Conor's life felt too big to handle. I knew our usual sisters' modus operandi of sharing the load of life's burdens had just taken a dramatic shift. I wondered if on some level my sister resented the fact that my children remained whole and their ability to pursue dreams unencumbered. And if the truth be told, I harbored guilt because this was happening to Conor, and the track of Kathy's existence was now altered forever. Although our sister relationship had never been based on jealousy, envy, or resentment, I'm certain there was a time or two my sister begrudged the fact that Conor's accident propelled her to a constant state of hardship, leaving me with the freedom to come and go from my "untouched" life. Yet, each day as I sat helpless by Kathy's side, my heart broke in places I never knew existed. I knew quite well this journey would be my sister's alone. All I could do was promise to be with her—completely.

ᕗ chapter 9 ᕗ

The morning after Neil cut his wrists, he drove from Nashville to Dayton and went directly to Kathy's house, where she and Gerry preceded his arrival. My sister remembers him walking into her home. His pupils were dilated, and he seemed void of emotion. Both she and Gerry were struck by the loss of his figurative footing. He walked into her family room; stumbling from exhaustion into her overstuffed chair. His wrists were wrapped in Band-Aids too small for the wounds inflicted by a kitchen knife. The reality was beyond comprehension. Here before them was Neil, the survivor, the one with nine lives, the brother who seemed unbreakable, now broken. He explained to them the course of recent events that led him to this place. He was matter-of-fact in his recollections, but full of clarity and insight regarding his recent pain.

Neil admitted the lung cancer diagnosis was a false story designed to provide justification for the death he had already planned for himself. Frantic preparations were arranged to help those left behind, especially Megan, the daughter he adored. The funeral had been pre-paid, his furniture placed in storage, and a cashier's check prepared her. All written directives were in a manila envelope sent via mail to Gerry's home. He calmly spoke of the moment while lying in his Nashville bathtub after slitting his wrists. His intention was to die, but as he sat there still lucid and physically functional, he glanced at nearby photos of our mom and Megan. He remembered the strength of the message resonating. *Get up and go home.* Somehow, despite the haze of a Benadryl and Coors Light hangover, he applied pressure to his wounds, slapped a few Band-Aids on his wrists and drove himself home to Dayton. Kathy recalled feeling she was in the midst of a bad dream.

Initially, we didn't spend too much time asking questions. We were cautious not to utter words that would add to his shame. The ensuing weeks were all about team-Grogan mobilization. Kathy opened her home to Neil, enveloping his rawness and brokenness with a blanket of family belonging. Home-cooked meals, invitations to high school track meets, and constant reminders of hope brought opportunities for Neil to renew himself through our love. Kathy thanked him for coming home. Gerry and I added to the conversations of hope and actively tried to create opportunities where abundance in being together outweighed the barrenness of his sorrows. We arranged family gatherings at which we encouraged him to seek counseling. We gave him books offering new perspectives on life. We shared our own vulnerabilities in order to comfort him. "You are not alone," we told him, regarding the sorrows and pain that threatened to hijack hope. Neil stayed with Kathy for several weeks. She tried to reach him: willing him, propelling him, and offering him a different perspective of what life still offered. She encouraged him to unravel the tightly wound internal tale he'd been telling himself for years—namely, that his worth was related to the worldliness of his possessions rather than the richness of his soul. She reminded him of the devastation we endured through Pat's death and our frustrations in not having been given the chance to help him. We believed we could have our helped our oldest brother choose life instead of death if only we'd known the depth of his despair. Neil knew as much as anyone the stinging pain from suicide.

Fragile as we all were, there was cause for renewed faith. Neil secured a new job in Dayton, signed a lease for an apartment, and brought his furniture out of storage. We were encouraged by the efforts made by him to craft a new beginning.

❧ chapter 10 ❧

Chicago

In the immediate aftermath of Conor's accident, we felt as if we were in the midst of rubble from the collapse of a former life. Just as immediate, however, was the recognition that we were leaning on grace, and felt a support often intangible and mysterious. Kathy and Phil held on during these agonizing days and nights of worry to threads of hope sewn with belief of God's presence. Perhaps it was a bit delusional to think Fr. Patrick, by way of his name, offered a direct celestial message from our brother Pat that Conor would be okay. Two months later, after Conor's transfer to the Rehabilitation Institute of Chicago, my sister's daily morning walk by Chicago's Museum of Contemporary Art became focal in placing her mindset. Skeptics might think it was crazy for her to think the museum's revolving sign, "MOTHER," was a direct encouragement from our mom. True, "MOTHER" was an advertisement for the current exhibition, but the infusion of strength my sister garnered from that sign helped set her day with a reminder of the permanency of her mom's love.

Not long after Conor's accident, Kathy pulled up on her iPad a paper Conor wrote for his Introduction to Christian Theology class at Loyola. Written just four months prior to his accident, *"Yahweh's First Symphony: The Harmony of Science and Religion,"* speaks of the communal relationship between scientific proof and supernatural existence in our universe. Conor wrote so eloquently about the energy source of God, which pervades the writings of the most respected and accomplished scientific thinkers' theories of life. It was a beautifully crafted paper that had an eerie foreboding. Conor, through his essay, was almost preparing us and himself for this journey by recognizing the vastness of God in all—I mean *all*—things. He wrote,

"According to Christianity we are the stewards of the earth, not only because the earth is a magnificent gift entrusted to us, but also, everything around us is, in fact, part of God. The water we drink, the air we breathe, the leaves that rustle in the wind, and the mountains that tower over the horizon are all part of God. In every breath that one takes, they are actually breathing in the same argon atoms, an inert atom, that Jesus Christ himself breathed. Everything that makes up the human body, and everything else, also at one time made up a star somewhere in the cosmos. We are fundamentally made up of, and thus connected to, the same things that make up everything around us. When Jesus was made fully human he allowed for all of physical reality to also become divine in its own existence. When we look down at our hands that pray, our legs that walk, and our arms that lift, once again we are seeing God.

Herein lies the biological evidence for the human trait of empathy; humans are hardwired to be their brother's keeper. Our body understands, maybe sometimes more than our minds do, that it is our responsibility, as part of this world, to help one another.

In light of these astounding proofs humans must accept their own reality: we are connected to the world around us, so we must be responsible for our actions, and likewise we are connected to everyone around us, so we must be responsible for our behavior. God was the source of all creation, Jesus made all matter divine, and humans are connected to it all; the unity of these things is the true harmony of Yahweh's First Symphony."

Conor's words propelled us forward, encouraging the quest to find meaning in everything. Kathy and Phil believed in the vast and encompassing Spirit whose generosity of love had no limit. In the songs we heard, in the name tags of restaurant servers, in cloud formations, or even in the stories we heard from others, everything was sifted through the lens of faith and encouragement. A stretch? Maybe. But for Kathy, desperation illuminated her belief in a broad and universal design which expanded her previous definition of faith. She needed to look no further than Conor's own words. With confidence in the healing synergy of the medical care, supernatural love, and collectivity of prayers, the symphony of God was consuming.

The first time my sister read "Yahweh's Symphony," Conor's insights regarding God blew her away. From the outset, through his words, Conor illuminated a path of reassurance for the rest of us that God was in every detail of this journey. Some days, though, Kathy had to work through excruciating pain and weariness, wondering when her prayers would be answered and how Conor could find his way back.

Fr. Patrick became Kathy's spiritual mentor. From the first encounter in the early morning hours of March 17, he offered gentle reminders that the symphony of grace was in concert mode. When my sister found herself sinking beneath fear or despair, Fr. Patrick seemed to instinctively know when to show up. Just days following Conor's admission, the overwhelming reality of his condition and the daunting possibilities for his recovery threatened to overthrow her commitment to hope. I called Fr. Patrick and asked him to come as my sister's challenge to reset her footing in faith was toughening. Her shoulders sank with fatigue from the ebb and flow of her son's condition. Her breath was desperate to find an inflow of hope, as Conor was not settling into a pattern of improvement she could hang on to.

The three of us sat in the family waiting room just outside the SICU. My sister held her face in her hands; her tears flowed with fear. The fatigue and worry were palpable as she simply asked Fr. Patrick for some counsel in how to even move forward in faith.

"Trust the medical team," Fr. Patrick began. His response struck me, as his method of spiritual counseling was not the kind of aloof disconnect some pastors offer. He didn't quote scripture, he didn't confuse the event further by saying this was God's will—that version of God we wanted nothing to do with. He also didn't burden Kathy further with advice on how to deepen her prayer routine. His accessible demeanor and strength in gentility would guide my sister time and time again. On this day, he reached directly into her fear and doubt.

He went to encourage Kathy to connect each worry-filled hour with the thread of confidence she had in Conor's caregivers. Indeed, my sister had complete assurance in the nurses, physicians, respiratory therapists, and social workers assigned to Conor. These highly trained professionals managed Conor's ever-changing condition with unyielding professionalism and skill. They were the Crippen's heroes. Kathy nodded her head. Yes, this made sense to her. Indeed, what she knew for sure was that she could trust the medical team.

Loyola's support for Conor and his family only intensified.

In addition to Fr. Patrick's frequent presence, Sr. Jean Delores Schmidt, Loyola's 93-year-old iconic basketball team chaplain joined Fr. Patrick in his early visits to see Conor. The two of them became Kathy and Phil's pastoral dynamic duo. Barely five feet tall, and exuding a spitfire spirit, Sr. Jean reminded Kathy of our mom with her optimism, bright smile, and sensible walking shoes. She navigated Loyola's campus and downtown streets of Chicago rivaling most people half her age. Fr. Patrick joked he could hardly keep up with her. When they both showed up, you knew a shot of optimism walked in the door. Sr. Jean was relentless in reminding Kathy of God's ability to take anything emotionally thrown at Him. Her counsel over the next months reminded Kathy of God's greatness and unyielding love for Conor. Fr. Patrick helped to place our impatience for Conor's improvement into the framework of "God's time." Always, Kathy felt renewed after their visits.

The concentric circles of encouragement expanded with those who were touched by Conor's story. Back home in Dayton, the outreach for Conor and his family was tremendous. Kathy received care packages from Alter High School, including handwritten notes from the students. Bracelets, necklaces, and tokens of trust were sent as tangible evidence that others were profoundly committed to helping the Crippens remain charged in faith. Conor's high school math teacher sent her the framed copy of a prayer she read aloud before each class. A parent whose son triumphed over cancer sent the religious medal he wore during chemotherapy treatment. Kathy and Phil were humbled by the instant and grand mobilization of support from their community. "Go Conor Go" signs soon adorned the walls of his SICU room. Even the SICU nursing staff joined in the movement hanging their own sign at the foot of Conor's bed.

The support from those we knew and strangers who cared became overwhelming for my sister. Being in a constant state of receiving was unnerving. As one who was much more comfortable with giving, the tremendous deluge became difficult for her. Each day, food arrived at the hospital café to feed those who were visiting. People showed up with prayer blankets, neighbors organized a community spring clean-up and landscaping renewal at the Crippen home. People we didn't even know sent cards, donated money, and were relentless in remaining in hope with the Crippens. The outpouring was incredible.

There were so few times Kathy allowed fear to surface, and so few people with whom she could share her trepidations. Fr. Patrick was one of them. His pop-in visits to the hospital offered Kathy the opportunity to shed her bravado. He offered consistent words that levitated her to new understanding. On one such visit, my sister was sharing with him how overwhelmed she was by the vast outreach. He reminded Kathy that sometimes, we just need to allow ourselves to receive. He went on to say that it's like when someone hugs you with all their might, and all you can do is stand there with your arms to your side. Humbling, yes, he told her, but there would come a time, he reminded, when Kathy will return the hug. I saw my sister's tears flow in humility, and I reminded her that she'd been hugging all her life.

Daily postings on Conor's Facebook page communicated not only his condition, but observations we had regarding our gratitude in the midst of anguish. I wrote about the simple graces that enabled my sister and her family to remain in the light of this very dark time. Others responded in kind, with inspirational stories of their own. PRFC became a stimulus for hope, which supported all of us who loved Conor. We synchronized rosary prayer services around the country. We felt the power of others choosing to believe this prayerful energy could really help make Conor better. The fact that these people would pause their hectic lives to gather in solidarity with Conor's intention taught us to broaden our trust. As Conor's condition moved deeper into graveness we were left with no other choice than to accept the lifeline that others were offering.

March 22, 2013 PRFC

As family and friends, we sit in the hospital café with water bottles, open bags of snacks, and NCAA basketball on the Loyola computers. It has been quite the day. Currently, Kathy and Phil are with Conor as Dr. Muro, the neurosurgeon, is placing a cranial shunt to help relieve some of the pressure that they have had such a challenge in managing. Bridget just reported, as Dr. Muro was describing to her the procedure and rationale for it, he then looked at her and told her, "Will you do me a favor when your brother wakes up? Since you're the oldest, will you kick his ass?" And in his slight chuckle, he communicated all the frustration, challenges, problem-solving, and down-right exasperation this medical team has experienced trying to get Conor's cranial pressure to just relax!!! So, we are not concerned as this is a minor procedure which will hopefully allow them to diminish the large amount of medication currently trying to control this situation. So please pray for success in that!!

In addition, the day has yielded so many blessings. Some of our family arrived and, along with Conor's loyal and stead-fast friends, we gathered again in the Chapel—led in prayer by Fr. Patrick. As we are further settling into the reality of this situation, gathering together gives us an opportunity to share, express gratitude, and remind one another of the presence of

God in all this. As Fr. Patrick said again today, God is very busy. He encouraged us to be present to these moments of God's presence in one another, in the team of caregivers, and most importantly, in Conor. We left the Chapel once again filled with more hope.

My sister shared with me earlier today that in the moments of despair that are still very present, she will take her phone and look at all your comments, your prayers, and your stories. She, along with the rest of us, gain strength from your words. Your words and this collective interaction of prayer soothe Kathy, Phil, Bridget, Jack, and those of us who love them so much.

Please continue to pray for decrease in cranial pressure and a more restful night not only for Conor, but for all his doctors and nurses that have worked so hard this day.

Conor's friends were constant. Loyola peers showed up every day, and friends from Alter High School made weekend trips to Chicago to offer support and encouragement. Visitors to Conor's room were restricted, but that didn't deter his gang from hanging out together in the hospital coffee shop which became home base for Conor supporters. None of this was surprising, for if you knew Conor, you knew the definition of loyalty and friendship. Conor belonged to this group. His friends brought their backpacks, did homework, and slouched into lounge chairs for hours at a time. They laughed together, chatted about their lives, and navigated their vigil with the greatest kind of hope: the promise of their own lives. Kathy and Phil were restored with the energy of their youth and mutual love for Conor. Their message was simple, "You've got this Crip."

Despite the startling situation of Conor's hospitalization, each day yielded awareness of an abundance of blessings. Fr.

Patrick encouraged us to be present to the moments of grace in one another, in the team of caregivers, and most importantly, in Conor.

Connection through Facebook became like an interactive prayer service. The hope for Conor translated into a scrapbook of messages and photos sent from all over the world. Pictures of people with makeshift signs—from the green bluffs of Ireland to the porch of a mission school in Guatemala—were sent via Facebook, providing daily doses of delight to Conor's darkened room. Kathy printed each photo and hung them on the walls and curtains surrounding him. Even celebrities joined in: Jack Hanna, Florida Georgia Line, and the winning jockey from Keeneland Race Course in Lexington held signs saying "Go Conor Go!" Hundreds of creative displays, from inscriptions in beach sand to letters made from matchbook cars to pennies to scrabble tiles, all offered support with fun and sometimes delightfully frivolous creativity. The outpouring was overwhelming and sustaining.

❧ chapter 11 ❧

Dayton—June, 2012

Following Neil's return, Gerry, Kathy and I did what we could to help him make a fresh start. I was with him the day he moved into his new apartment. I helped him line his kitchen cabinets with shelf paper before placing his plates and glasses in order. We adhered felt pads to his furniture legs to guard the hardwood floors from scratching. We decided which photos to hang on the wall. Our family was confident in Neil's renewed possibilities, and we loved that he was living nearby.

Kathy invited Neil to Conor's and Jack's high school track meets. He met Gerry for beers, came to my house for meals, was in contact with at least one of us every day. The four of us went out to dinner. I felt the comfort of being together. We weren't afraid to talk with him about his sadness, or encourage him to design a plan for new dreams. It felt good that we were strong once again in hope. *Never again.*

It was June 19, 2012, and the sun rose amidst a cloudless sky. Brilliance reigned, maybe by design. We Grogans needed illumination as a new darkness descended. Despite all our supporting efforts, we knew that there would come a day when Neil would have to look into his own soul to on take on the challenge of self-renewal. We could only do so much to help him. The ultimate responsibility to heal himself was his, and his alone.

The inevitable discomfort for Neil to take an honest look at himself made us all realize his journey to contentment was far from complete, but we were still optimistic. In truth, the "muscles" of self-actualization had atrophied for his 57-year-old mind. Perhaps he was unable to distinguish his bruised ego from his authentic self. Perhaps the road to recovery seemed arduous or lost. Perhaps the despair of his soul shielded his ability to see the goodness and light within himself. Perhaps he just wasn't able. This day, June 19, would be his day of self-reckoning.

The phone rang at 6:50 a.m. It was my sister. In the aftermath of my mom's recent death, the shrill of the ring interrupted my dream state. Automatically, I thought my mom must have fallen again, as she did repeatedly in the months before she died. I wasn't quite awake to reality as I reached for the phone. It wasn't unusual for Kathy and I call each other when my mom needed help: together, it was easier.

In those times, I would quickly rise out of bed, dress in whatever clothes were left over from the day before, and drive to my parents' home, just minutes from my house. I offered a repeated prayer to help me prepare for whatever I would find upon arrival. I admit to being selfishly relieved when I would see my sister's car in the driveway. It meant Kathy, as first responder, would already have assessed and buffered the scene.

Would it be a simple slide to the floor that left our 80-year-old mom laughing in embarrassment? Would there be another pool of blood on the carpet after hitting her head on the bedside table? Would my dad be hyperventilating and chewing his lip in distress? Would my mom need to be immediately bathed and bedsheets changed, due to her bladder release? All these triggers flooded my mind as I heard Kathy's voice on the line; once again unprepared for another emergency.

"Anne," she said with alarm, "we have to get over to Neil's. I think he's trying it again."

I was jarred to wakefulness. Of course, this wasn't about my mom. Dread overcame me.

I drove to Neil's apartment, trying to prepare myself. I called Mark who was already on his way to work. I called Gerry. He, too, was on his way. I called Kathy. No answer. My mind was racing. Perhaps he was feeling unsteady again and needed our help. This time, I told myself, we'd insist he stick with a treatment plan. All I could say was "Oh my God!" over and over again in the car, almost as a centering prayer. I felt my insides quake and my heart plummet, as if tethered to a boulder sinking in the vast ocean. I tried to deepen my breath. Surely this could not be happening a second time.

A few seconds later, my sister called me.

My beating heart felt there was no room in my chest. "What's going on?"

"Anne," she cried. "He's gone."

"What do you mean, where'd he go?" I felt hysteria rising.

"He's gone," she repeated over and over again, sobbing in resignation.

I turned the corner to the street where Neil lived. I saw my sister sitting on the pavement. Her car door was still open, keys in the ignition, as if time stopped cold. My bewilderment shifted; reluctant clarity was setting in. I ran to Phil, dressed in suit and tie for what was supposed to be a usual day at the office. He embraced me, repeating the futile words in my ear.

"Anne, I am so sorry…so, so sorry."

No, I thought to myself. *Not again. Please no!*

Gerry was standing with a police officer. Fire engines, police cars, and EMT vehicles circled Neil's driveway, but there was little activity. It was over. Neil died by a self-inflicted gunshot wound. And just like that, another brother was gone. I went to Gerry, hoping he could tell me this was all wrong; a mistake. His arms encircled me, and I felt his tears melt onto my cheek. Neil was gone.

Over years of family difficulties, Gerry was the one we all called in times of crisis. He embodied a centered demeanor and measured ability to problem-solve. My mom called him "the rock." She leaned on Gerry for all things great or trite. Whether the kitchen garbage disposal needed fixing or crisis hit, he showed up. When Pat's bipolar disorder exacerbated or suffered breakdowns due to the demons taunting his soul, it was Gerry who accompanied my mom to the hospital psychiatric ward. His brotherly embrace made everything better, until now. Under this cloudless sunny sky, Gerry was called, again, to lead us through the darkness.

While the rest of us were aimlessly pacing Neil's front yard, I noticed my only surviving brother sitting on Neil's back patio in a cushioned lawn chair. He was hunched over with one hand holding a cell phone to his ear, with his forehead resting in his other hand. My heart broke all over again. I knew Gerry was calling Megan, and I felt sadness take on new definition. At age 26, young adults should be preparing for great new beginnings. Instead, on this day in June, Megan's world shattered.

I felt the sour taste of bile burn my throat as I witnessed Gerry informing Meg her dad was gone by his own choosing. She tried so hard to lift his soul in the months preceding his death, knowing he was struggling. Just days before, Neil and Megan enjoyed kayaking on the Chicago River. His last weekend was spent with her, yet his silent goodbye remained tucked in secrecy. She had no clue.

Gerry then called Michael, forever marked by his dad's suicide. Now faced with the loss of the one who assumed a fatherly role, Michael was propelled again into the anguish, trying to understand how someone so loved could choose to go away. In the years since Pat's death, I've screamed to the heavens in confusion and bewilderment. Pat would have found such joy in watching Michael grow up, create his own family, and work hard to successfully build his own business. He would have seen himself in his son: the high-pitched giggle, the strong and tender hands, and the gentle and inviting demeanor. As Michael's life journey moved on without his dad, the rise of frustration and anger surfaced over and over again because Pat, quite simply, was missing out on goodness. If only Pat could have held on. And now, Neil.

After the emergency personnel left and Neil's body was taken away, we entered his home looking for clues. We found his worn Birkenstock sandals on the floor in the kitchen where he last kicked them off. We found his ashtray on the back porch, filled with cigarette butts. Coors beer cans stocked the refrigerator. There were random coins and breath mints next to a half-full jar of cashews sitting on the kitchen counter.

We each took some time to wander Neil's home. I felt as if I was violating his privacy as we searched through his desk drawer, rummaged through his closets, and thumbed through his cell phone, looking for insight to understand how he could finally leave us. We all sank into the not-yet-worn couch and chairs in his family room where just a few weeks prior, Neil hosted us for dinner. That night we gathered in celebration of his new home, realizing he was still fragile but confident in his ability to overcome his anguish. On this June morning we sat together, asking questions that had no answers. We lingered together feeling the spirit of Neil in this place he tried to call home. Leaving the apartment meant we would leave him behind forever.

Gerry, Kathy, and I held on to one another as we navigated the painful weeks and months following this second surreal loss. How could two brothers in the same family die by suicide? We began our sibling unit with five, and now we were three. The disbelief and enormity of loss was overwhelming. The only way we could cope was to remain connected. We were still Grogan strong; sharing the emotional survival kit in unison.

Six months following Neil's death, we rang in 2013 with the belief that we'd endured enough. We were hopeful in thinking our family had tapped out suffering. It was time to regroup. We were still working through our grief from losing Neil and my mom, but we looked forward to more ordinary days where the rhythm of routine could help us to heal together. Little did we know how shortsighted our feelings of entitlement would be.

chapter 12

Chicago

It was Palm Sunday morning: one week since Conor's accident and the start of Holy Week. I was cognizant of the parallels between Christ's journey of the cross and Conor's challenge to regain life. This Palm Sunday it felt as if Conor and his family were carrying their own cross. I thought about the connection my sister now had with Mary. A mother's pain is uniquely intense when privy to her child's unimaginable trauma. Mary, like Kathy, was challenged with seeking reason and purpose as she witnessed her son's fate, unaware of the new life to come. The uncertainty of Conor's outcome was happening in real time, every minute defined by the looming fears. Unlike the Gospel accounts of Christ's journey, we had no guaranteed resurrection chapter, and nothing more to hold on to than our sheer belief that Conor had to be okay. He just had to. We felt as if Neil owed us this.

Phil and Bridget left Chicago early that morning to return home. Jack had school obligations, and he needed his dad. Bridget had her last round of semester finals at Xavier University, where she was scheduled to graduate in a few short weeks. I remained with Kathy.

Dr. Muro came in early to do his daily rounds. He wore his wool coat and cashmere scarf with iPod earbuds hanging from the inside collar of his coat. His reputation preceded him. You can tell the competency of physicians by the recommendations of the staff members who work beside them. A Northwestern-trained neurosurgeon, Dr. Muro was praised by the SICU nurses who witnessed his skill firsthand.

Dr. Muro stood by Conor's bed that morning, watching the monitors. We could the see wheels of thought turning through his furrowed brow. Accustomed to multi-daily visits by him to manage Conor's fluid condition, Kathy had developed a connection with him that surpassed your average physician-patient relationship. My sister didn't know how to rest at shallowness with anyone, much less the physician in charge of saving her son. As always, she tried to probe him for "something good." Yet his words were few. His cashmere scarf came off, followed by his coat, which he hung on the metal arm of Conor's monitor. We sat in silence, wishing not to disrupt his thought process by asking questions, so we waited for some indication of his concern. Why wasn't he talking? What was he thinking? Dr. Muro appeared so pensive. I honestly thought Conor was doing better. His cranial pressure numbers were lingering in the 20's. Wasn't that what they wanted?

After what seemed like an eternity, Dr. Muro looked at my sister told her in a very direct way what needed to be done: Bilateral Decompressive Craniectomy. He then used both his hands and placed them on either side of his head, providing a visualization of where he would perform surgery. Literally, he wanted to remove Conor's skull.

Taken aback but ever calm, Kathy paused, then asked for explanation and reasoning. Dr. Muro took a seat in the chair next to her. With a pen and the back of a random get-well card envelope, he drew a rough sketch of what the surgical procedure entailed. Two hand-sized bone flaps would be removed from Conor's head and placed inside the skin layers of his lower abdomen. Storing the cranial plates within Conor's belly would keep them viable so his body would recognize them as his own when surgically replaced, minimizing the chance for rejection. It would take eight weeks for the swelling in Conor's brain to fully subside. In the meantime, Conor would wear a protective helmet to guard his unshielded brain. Dr. Muro said Conor's brain pressure was not trending in the way he wanted, and the risk for irreparable damage was too great. This surgery, he felt, was necessary.

Kathy told him that just months earlier, Conor was excited to learn about this "new procedure" whereby a part of the skull could be removed and stored within the body following severe brain injury. Conor and Kathy marveled about the recovery of Rep. Gabby Giffords, the Congressional Representative from Arizona. Following brain trauma resulting from gun violence in 2011, she had this same surgery, offering the cutting-edge chance for survival. This felt serendipitous to my sister. She recalled how she and Conor used to talk about what would happen if one side of his brain didn't work for some reason. Jill Bolte Taylor's book, *My Stroke of Insight*, was one of Conor's favorite books as he was fascinated by the story of Taylor's own stroke and subsequent understandings of how the left and right sides of the brain work in tandem. Conor was fascinated by the brain; yet here he was, the subject of the very same innovative and delicate brain surgery he'd been excited to learn about mere months ago.

Dr. Muro confidently explained the surgery and my sister remained brave within her despair. I witnessed an unspoken connection between them. The intimate scene unfolded between a brilliant neurosurgeon and dedicated mother. As Dr. Muro offered a chance for recovery, Kathy needed to speak to Conor's promising place in this world. Dr. Muro listened to her, a testament to their mutual admiration. Kathy signed the consent form—a scribbled signature laced with trust. He put his arm around my sister's slumped shoulders and reassured her. She placed her head on his shoulder, allowing a few tears to flow. Herein rested the cultivated bond of trust between them. If Dr. Muro could allow potential for Conor's recovery, Kathy could take over with the mission to do whatever was necessary to heal him with love. I was reminded of my mom's worry for Kathy. As she gave Dr. Muro permission for the surgery, I could only imagine the loneliness and isolation she felt. As much as I knew she needed me next to her, I knew she needed Phil more. All I could do was remain by her side and catch the silences of her worry.

I thought that day, and often since then, of Dr. Muro. What was supposed to be Sunday morning hospital rounds turned into an all-day commitment. During the frequent visits to Conor's bedside since admission to the SICU, and because of my sister's engagement, Dr. Muro spoke of his wife, his two young children, and the woes of housetraining two new puppies. This Palm Sunday may very well have included family plans, but his family carried on without him. As the wife of a dedicated physician, I sent a silent wish to his wife and children. I hoped somehow, they knew our appreciation for him also included gratitude for their understanding.

Suddenly, the room held a flurry of anesthesiologists, respiratory therapists, surgical nurses, and countless other hospital personnel preparing Conor for surgery. In the mist of the ordered chaos, my sister fell to her knees at Conor's bedside. The composure while talking with Dr. Muro gave way to desperation as she cried, buried her cheek against the softness of her son's hands; kneading his fingers in her frantic need for him to be okay.

She spoke to him, reminded him of his dreams to visit Dubai, climb Mt. Kilimanjaro, and attend more Dave Matthews Band concerts. She told him Bridget and Jack needed him. She spoke to him with confidence that he could hear her, despite his comatose state. Her longing was palpable. She was willing him and pleading in her attempts to reach the spirit of her son buried deep amidst his brokenness.

The deepest capillaries of my being bled for my sister. I couldn't believe that in just one week, her ordinary world had been hijacked by this random and senseless accident. Just over a week ago, Kathy and Phil were out to dinner, choosing a nice bottle of wine and dreaming about their eminent days of empty nesting. Brain trauma lived in another world then, but defined their lives now.

There is an eeriness in a surgical waiting room on a Sunday afternoon. Weekdays bring a collection of worried loved ones who gather with coffee and crosswords waiting to hear the report of a successful surgery. The receptionist's chair is occupied with a hospital volunteer in her yellow smock providing updates to various family members, or directing them to the nearest restroom. The television blares the high volume of game-show exuberance. On this Sunday afternoon, except for the few of us vested in Conor, the room was darkened. The overhead lights were dim. The television screen was in sleep mode. The empty receptionist's chair was pushed underneath the paperless desk. It felt unnerving as we gathered to wait amidst such a barren scene.

They say there is strength in numbers, and our small group in this otherwise-abandoned waiting room felt mighty. Along with Kathy and me, there were companions who provided support, prayer, and camaraderie in the afternoon's slow passage of time. Casey Dentino, Conor's study pal from Loyola, and Keenan remained with us for the duration; their overstuffed backpacks flung to the side of the waiting room chairs. They told stories of Conor at Loyola, laughing at recollections of "Crip" tales. Julie Jung, my sister's best friend since grammar school, came from her home in Normal, Illinois. Her presence provided the unspoken comfort from one whose kinship embodied a lifetime of support.

My daughter Kate, a high school English teacher in Bloomington, Indiana, was on her Spring Break. She and Megan made their way to the chapel to pray. Neither of these cousin-in-compatriots remembered how to say the rosary prayers despite their Catholic upbringing, but somehow it didn't matter. With the help of Google, they made it through in desperate prayer for their cousin. Having Megan there was a reminder that we were a family of survivors. Her resilience was infectious.

We spent the afternoon of this Palm Sunday together, the lone group in the surgical waiting area. We laughed and told stories as we huddled together. This was not our first experience with surgical waiting rooms. Memories of Neil, Gerry, Kathy, and me passing time while our mom endured numerous surgeries supported our ability to navigate the worrisome afternoon with usual protocol. Our coping strategies had been in place for years: we laughed, we played "20 questions," we shared ordinary conversation to keep our anxiety at bay, and we allowed silence to store our angst. Sequential Hail Marys and Our Fathers were recited together, followed by reminiscing with iconic, lighthearted family stories. The heaviness of the surgical reality—Dr. Muro removing Conor's skull—tempted despair, but the power to resist came from our confidence in him, one another, and the cultivated trust we were compelled to believe in.

The surgery lasted almost six hours. Although our energy was measured for most of this time, we began to get anxious as dusk blanketed the Chicago skies. Just when our impatience piqued, Dr. Muro sauntered through the surgery department's automatic double doors wearing surgical scrubs. His dark hair was matted from hours of wearing his surgical cap. He plopped down in the waiting room chair across from Kathy, chewing ice from a Styrofoam cup. Slouching with his legs crossed, Dr. Muro exuded a casualness one would never expect after removing a skull and tucking it into someone's abdomen. I guess it was just another day in the operating room; but for us, it was monumental. It seemed like an eternity before he spoke.

"Well?" Kathy finally said.

Dr. Muro spoke with confidence, simply stating that everything was fine, as if he'd stitched a cut knee. I suppose it is the upshot of brilliance when expertise becomes mundane. His relaxed demeanor (we laughed about it later) indicated he did his job, did it well; and was enjoying his cup of ice. I thought, well, if he's calm, then we should be too. Dr. Muro gave needed details of the surgery and Kathy expressed appreciation. Her confidence in him so tenderly expressed hours earlier were fruitful. Post-surgery, Conor's ICP level was 3. That was good news.

This particular Palm Sunday, we did not read the Gospel narratives of Christ's passion. In fact, we were quite distracted from the ritual of putting ourselves into the company of Christ's journey. We were engrossed in our own Passion that day, tethering worry with faith. It would take another 48 hours before Conor's ICP permanently stabilized, but eventually the relief of successful surgery brought an end to the critical state of Conor's brain pressure. We dared hope for more measured days bringing the possibilities for improvement.

Later that evening, knowing Conor was settled, we all decompressed together. I observed Kathy and Megan with new light.

There was a poetic and beautiful connection between them—one of which they were probably not aware. Despite the trials my sister had endured thus far in her life, she was navigating the most challenging. When I looked at Megan, I saw the resilience born from the call to courage; far beyond her years. I couldn't help but remember her poise in the aftermath of her dad's death.

Following Neil's suicide, we tried to memorialize him with celebration, but it was tough. Again, Neil prepaid his funeral expenses. The memorial service was to be performed at the funeral home, by request. This time, there would be no refund.

We were met at the entrance by two elderly men in black suits. I could barely hear their mumbled condolences as I walked through the double doors. Dread preceded my walk down the hallway toward the room where Neil's body lay. I had to keep reminding myself he was really gone as I walked the corridor, gaining strength from those who were with me, and especially from Gerry, who would continue to lead us. Megan insisted the casket be open for family, so that she could see her dad one more time. She needed closure in this agonizing nightmare. My legs shook in the anticipation of seeing my brother, gone. Yet there was Megan, driven by poise and courage. Nothing, however, could have prepared me for what I saw as I turned the corner and entered the long, floral arrangement lined pathway to his casket.

There was my Neil, my brother, lying in state. Unlike the peace and restoration of beauty seen in my mom as she lay open for us to see following her death, there was nothing good about seeing Neil dead. His dark gray suit didn't fit right. He never wore suits anyway. My very trim brother had developed a protruding belly, unbecoming to his bike-rider body. And then there was the baseball cap, placed to hide trauma from his gunshot. The image before me was so radically different than the brother I knew: always so full of vivacious energy. Surely his essence was hiding somewhere, but I couldn't see it.

I was in awe of Megan as she showed no fear or hesitation. Her love for her father transcended the distorted image before her, and she was able to embrace him in a way that humbled my need to turn away. I hung on to Mark as Gerry and Kathy took their own time to reconcile the image of our brother. And my poor, old dad, who couldn't even begin to understand any of this, just kept whispering, "Neil doesn't look very good." Yet even he was not afraid to approach the casket to whisper parting words of love. I couldn't do it.

Megan chose to close the casket for the public service. I was relieved and more comfortable remembering Neil from the images of our hearts rather than that which lay beneath the casket top. Several of us took turns eulogizing. Words were spoken of his place in our family: his ability to fill the brokenness of any situation with new hope and laughter. We remembered his metaphorical role as the wind; his ability to blow into our lives, bringing new vitality that reminded us of the strength of our family.

Michael spoke of the power of depression. He equated the intensity of such despair to being at the bottom of a well, surrounded in darkness with no ladder and no one able to hear cries for help—a description he felt his own dad must have experienced. Michael's words were poignant, and his remarks solidified the bond he and Megan would forever share.

The afternoon continued with tributes and condolences from so many who loved Neil. We plowed through the long hours at the funeral home aided by a shot or two of Irish Whiskey stashed in the coat room. Despite the tragedy of losing Neil, our family held on to one another, surrounded Megan with support, and found a way to celebrate—even amidst this inconceivable loss.

Megan was the last to speak. Her fortitude and composure commanded the room. She thanked everyone for coming,
acknowledged her anger with her dad, and spoke with pride of
her father and the importance he would continue to hold. Her
strength was reminiscent of my mom, who had been the para-
mount example of how to navigate troubled times with grace
and style.

A few days following Neil's funeral, Megan packed her
Volkswagen Beetle with those things she could not part with:
her dad's comforter, his pillow, his CD collection, and photos
that told the story of their close relationship. This was not an easy
day. I stood by his kitchen table, waiting for Megan to absorb
one final connection amidst her dad's belongings. I glanced down
to the floor, and there were Neil's worn Birkenstock sandals,
still where he'd left them. There are no guidelines to grief, and
gut-wrenching loss can resurface with haste that is suffocating.
I found myself sinking with sadness. I walked Megan to her car
full of relics forced to be part of her past. I waved goodbye as she
set off on the road back to Chicago. Alone, she was charged with
carving a new path for herself. Her forever companion would be
heartache and loss. I tried not to be angry with Neil for leaving
her, but it was hard.

Megan's residence in Chicago was laced with a weird sort of
poetic justice, grounded in the aftermath of these two family
tragedies. Megan and her apartment, just blocks from Advocate
Illinois Masonic Hospital, became our resting place as we took
turns helping Kathy and Phil keep vigil at Conor's bedside. Those
of us coming and going slept on her couch, processed the intense
days with a late-night glass of wine, and depended on her while
navigating this unforeseen journey. Megan became an anchor for
my sister. Her daily visits, bringing optimism in her smile and

possibility from the world beyond Conor's bedside, provided a lifeline.

Megan would have embraced the chance to love her dad toward wellness. Sudden death robs us of the opportunity to rally or mobilize. In the end, no one could have saved him, but there was hope for Conor. His story, unlike Neil's, could be one of restoration and healing. Still raw with anguish, Megan chose to cloak Kathy and Phil with the byproduct of her own grief journey: mutual love for Neil and the chance to be part of hope, where rebuilding of life was possible. Our choice to believe that Conor's accident somehow provided the opportunity for healing in the aftermath of Neil's passing certainly made nothing right about Neil's death, nor acceptable about Conor's injury. But the potential for good was rising, and for that we were grateful.

Sitting in the presence of these two admired women, I realized both of them were born of the same cloth as my mom. Despite the tragic trajectory thrust upon them, both of them stood taller and became strong advocates for determination and the power of love to reign. I was humbled to be with them both.

❧ chapter 13 ❧

Chicago

It was Easter Sunday. For two weeks, Conor lay in the SICU navigating his way through a precarious fight for life. In the aftermath of his cranial surgery, we finally felt there was possibility for reprieve. Conor's ICP was well within normal range. He seemed stable enough for Kathy and Phil to leave the hospital for a few hours to attend Easter Mass at Loyola's Madonna della Strada Chapel. The sun's brilliant luster amidst the cloudless sky promised the certainty of Spring. Mark and our daughter Holly arrived from Dayton, and along with Megan and Conor's friends, we gathered in celebration.

Sr. Jean met us at the entrance to the Chapel with her infectious smile and encompassing embrace; setting the mood for Easter joy. Keenan reserved the front two pews, so the Crippens settled in with prime seats. Angelic voices opened the morning's celebration as choir harmonies filled the church with songs of renewal. The stained-glass windows came alive by virtue of the sun. Vibrant colors illuminated the chapel as light rays filtered with unapologetic optimism. Fr. Patrick flanked the opening procession as celebrant. Grace overflowed.

That Easter Sunday, March 31, 2013 PRFC

I sit in a quiet mode, challenged to find the words to describe our Easter thus far. First and most important, Conor is doing well. Another restful day in anticipation for a hopeful week. Blood count numbers are better, slowly weaning off more sedatives, and docs and nurses are pleased.

Within this context of believing that we will soon navigate our way toward more response from him, we have shared, as family, an extraordinary day. It is a beautiful bright day here in Chicago, reminding us that the promise of spring whispers. As a family, we all celebrated Easter Mass in the beautiful chapel at Loyola. We brought to the altar today hope and intention for Conor, and we left filled to capacity with the Spirit. The resounding choir and organ accompaniment filled us to the brim with joy rising. From the opening song to the closing procession, the music alone serenaded God's presence in everything. Of course, when we saw Fr. Patrick emerge from the sacristy clothed as celebrant, we were again reassured of God's hope. And of course, the beauty of the chapel itself makes you think God lives there.

I believe the entire Mass was an intentional prayer for Conor. Fr. Patrick spoke of the Crippens and Conor in tandem (again) with the mystery of the empty tomb and all the varied questions, heartache, and all that is just part of the story. We sat as family, feeling enveloped in a love that, again, felt transcending. If there could be an Easter celebration in a church which communicated a tangible, specific, and hopeful message, today was it. And I believe that God's beautiful and sure voice of this morning, which was spoken in this collective way, meets the promise of who Conor is called to be. We are willing participants of this grace-filled journey for this incredible young man we have always known is just plain great.

We then transformed the hospital café (now called the Crippen café) to our Easter banquet room. Repositioning tables, we sat together in a familiar way: as family in celebration and abundance. We took a picture so that we could share with Conor what we did this Easter. We toasted to him, to one another, and to this journey that will forever change each one of us. We all agreed that Conor is leading the way so that all of us can eventually give back all we have been given.

I sit here humbly surrounded by family, visitors, and all of you in spirit, overwhelmed by the meaning of this Easter. We are grateful for so much…

Despite Conor's lingering coma, we rode the wave of gratefulness. His condition, thus far, had been defined by cranial pressure, and now that his brain was no longer stressed by swelling, we could all breathe again. We chose to rest in momentary joy even though Conor was exhibiting no sign of consciousness. He remained unresponsive to any of the expressions of love around him. He was still on life support unable to even open his eyes. The scars from his skull flap removal were still fresh. Staple sutures bilaterally lined the sides of his shaven head. There was still plenty to worry about, but for a few hours on this brilliant Easter Sunday we borrowed hope from the story of the tomb, allowing respite from the expanding challenges ahead. We decided to create an Easter celebration like no other. Moving a few tables and chairs, we created one big long table in the café where we could all sit together in fellowship and gladness.

Mark walked the nearby streets of Chicago in search of a Honey Baked Ham. Megan refined her rookie culinary skills by making potato casserole and dessert. We used paper plates, plastic utensils, and created a banquet table of family cohesiveness.

Conor continued to lie in his fourth-floor bed. So much remained unknown; but what we did know was that he'd survived the past two weeks, and collectively we were looking forward to the realm of his rehabilitation. We toasted to Conor's resilience, to his example of how to survive, and to one another. I was so grateful that my sister was given this Easter to reset herself in hope. And although there would be more Holy Week journeys, this Easter reminded us that resurrection was possible, even in real life.

. . . . .

Our celebration provided a light reprieve as joy temporarily outweighed fear. With Conor's skull flaps safely tucked beneath the skin of his lower belly, stability reigned. Now, it was time to think about the next step. Rehabilitation was a big word, given the comprehensive nature of his deficits. Over the next week, his wean from sedatives and anesthetic medication meant Conor could open his eyes, but otherwise he remained unresponsive. His stare was vacant, lost in the abyss of brain injury. He was breathing on his own but could not walk, stand, or even sit by himself. What caused the most heartache was Conor's inability to hold his head up; instead, his chin hung to his chest. He appeared listless, but we believed his capacity for insight and awareness were inside his damaged neurons somewhere. The question loomed in how to access the vibrant, fun-loving young man we all adored. The plastic feeding tube inserted into his stomach facilitated liquid nutrition, but otherwise, he was totally dependent. The thought of even where to begin was daunting.

After an angst-filled discussion of whether or not to bring Conor back to Ohio for recovery, Kathy and Phil decided to investigate the Rehabilitation Institute of Chicago,[3] an inpatient

[3] In March 2017, the Rehabilitation Institute of Chicago became the Shirley Ryan Ability Lab.

rehab facility whose reputation was prestigious. *U.S. News & World Report* ranked the RIC as #1—the best rehabilitation facility in the world—consistently since 1991. Indeed, Conor's most promising chance for rebirth was just down the road from Illinois Masonic, but still so far away from home. Continued family separation and Kathy and Phil's parallel living became secondary as the fight for Conor's wellness occupied all facets of priority.

An RIC physician came for an assessment to determine whether Conor was appropriate for their rehab unit. After all, there needed to be somewhere to begin. The physician was looking for some kind of connection with Conor; some capacity to respond on command in attempt to identify some sort of baseline. The evaluation did not last long, because Conor basically flunked the test. She asked him to look left, look right. She asked him to give her a thumbs-up or blink his eyes if he could hear her. Nothing. His head hung, listless. The physician told Kathy she had "concerns" about Conor's inability to follow any commands. Believing that Conor, even in his comatose state, could hear and absorb the skeptical energy of her words, Kathy asked the RIC representative to step out so they could talk openly in the waiting room.

Kathy sensed this woman was about to tell her that Conor didn't meet the benchmark for admission due to poor prognosis. Images of Conor's willpower flooded her mind. As a senior in high school, during a track team practice, Conor wanted to prove to the coach he could break the school record for number of consecutive 200-meter sprints run in the course of one practice. He then went on to run 42 of them, barely able to walk afterwards. His capacity for willpower made him unstoppable when he put his mind to it. Kathy was certain that his fortitude would rise again, despite his current state.

Before Kathy allowed the physician to formulate words of rejection, she enlightened the doctor with testimony of his determination, his passion for learning, his quest for life meaning and competitive spirit. Kathy spoke of Conor's exceptional achievements and ability to work hard. She pleaded her case that Conor mattered in the world, and that he would use this journey to better the lives of others. She directly asked the doctor to give him a chance. Once he was healed enough to take control of his own recovery, she said through her tears, he would defy all odds.

Kathy appealed with passion, noticing the physician's facial expression soften and eyes fill with tears. Their eyes connected, and my sister seized on the opportunity to infiltrate the doctor's clinical mind with her heart knowledge of Conor's capabilities. Conor had a purpose, she said. All roads of his life led to this point, she added. Kathy shed tears in her desperation for Conor to be given this chance. The clinical realities of Conor's state were met with a mother's overriding belief that Conor could overcome this catastrophic injury. Kathy allowed no space between the doubt of professional expertise and her trust in Conor's potential. In an apparent about-face, the doctor agreed to recommend Conor for admission to the RIC.

My sister was left shaking in the aftermath of her meeting. She felt herself collapse into the realities that were looming. There would be nothing easy about the road that lie ahead, yet she was settling into the role of Conor's advocate. Impressing even herself, she recognized her growing awareness; she needed to be audacious in her mission to save her son. Kathy was rising up, no longer able to sit at Conor's bedside and depend on others to care for him. In the weeks and months to come, she stepped up again and again to convince professional skeptics of Conor's potential.

I continued to write daily updates for Conor's Facebook page. The uplifting response from thousands of followers had a definite correlation to the tone of Conor's story: one of active and stubborn faith. Stories of hope and renewal were laced with a constant call to believe that even on the worst day, the cup was half full. Dedication to believe in the power of optimism is not a story for the faint-hearted. There was a great divide between the poor clinical forecast of independent living and Kathy's faith in her son. Conor had already defied the odds by merely surviving, and my sister's ferocious armor was being polished for battle. Yes, her voice was gaining strength, but the seam of her grit was not without the leak of fears and tears. On those days, all I could do was sit by her side and believe enough for the both of us.

Kathy and Phil scheduled a tour of the RIC. I could tell anxiety was building for my sister. Her self-imposed exile within the confines of the SICU protected her from the outside world. For weeks, she encased herself in the security of Conor's room. She allowed herself to only think about the hours that connected each day. In addition, the relationships with the medical staff fostered a family environment where Kathy felt safe and cared for. Now that medication drips and monitor alarms were tapering, she was forced to think about life beyond Illinois Advocate Masonic Hospital. That, for Kathy, was terrifying.

There were a few times when the positive and hopeful words I wrote on Conor's Facebook page did not reflect the intense heartache and overwhelming challenge of Conor's situation. Kathy and Phil's first encounter with the 10th floor of the RIC was, in some ways, even more difficult than that fateful night of the accident.

✦ chapter 14 ✦

Chicago

The RIC is located near the Northwestern Medical Center, just off Michigan Avenue in downtown Chicago. My sister recalls walking through the revolving doors into the lobby; it was the first time she caught a glimpse into the longevity of TBI recovery.

Kathy and Phil took the elevator to the 10th floor, dedicated to brain trauma. Prior to now, Kathy refused to characterize Conor as typical in brain injury. Photos of other TBI victims portrayed blank stares and a dimness reflected in their eyes. Conor was different, she insisted. Yet, seeing the patients of the 10th floor, some sitting wheelchairs appearing almost catatonic felt like a tidal wave of truth that came crashing into Kathy and Phil's fragile hearts of hope. Conor, in reality, was no different. The common room showed caregivers walking in sweat pants and slippers to the lounge to refill their coffee cups indicating this was their home away from home. Although she knew they had no other choice, my sister had a hard time visualizing Conor here. Rehabilitation needed to begin, but it didn't look pretty.

Those who suffered trauma or strokes were treated on this unit with a multitude of therapies designed to reignite impaired brain function. Kathy and Phil toured the impressive therapy rooms and met physical, speech, and occupational therapists. They were versed on research being conducted, the medical staff, and the multitude of support therapies.

The consequence of this move was sobering. Constant attention by SICU staff would be replaced by hands-on family care in preparation for return to home. No longer would Kathy and Phil sit idly by while others ministered to the details of their son's life. Now, they would become active participants in therapeutic exercises, bathing, and grooming. The insulation of the SICU room would be replaced with the charge of a lifetime: that of bringing their son back to life.

Following the tour, my sister remembered the shell shock of the visit. Visualizing Conor on this inpatient unit left Kathy and Phil wondering if he could overcome his injury. Exiting the RIC, Kathy and Phil found a windless, sun-patched area on the side of a nearby building off Michigan Avenue, sat in the grass, and tried get a grip on what rehabilitation really meant. They sat in silence, Kathy resting her weariness on Phil's tense shoulder and trying to regain footing on the reality of where Conor needed to be. The visual of patients with brain injury yielded doubt and skepticism for the first time since March 17. This next phase was more than either of them could comprehend. They were overwhelmed. Weathered by the SICU phase, my sister was charged again to outmaneuver her fatigue and rise up in belief that healing was possible. Fr. Patrick's advice many weeks prior rang with new meaning. Kathy and Phil were charged, once again, with trusting the medical staff: specifically, the RIC 10th-floor therapists.

Kathy called Mark. "Tell me he's going to get through this," she pleaded. "Tell me this is possible. Tell me I'm not crazy. Tell me he can be okay again. Tell me he can recover." The litany of her desperate pleas erupted from shaken confidence. She needed

Mark's professional reassurance and familiar encouragement. Their relationship, cultivated over years, reflected not only love for me, but genuine concern and love for one another. Kathy respected and needed his valued and trusted opinion. Mark, despite his own deep reservation, met my sister in her doubt and lifted her with words of support.

"Kath," he said with tender authority, "Conor can do this. He *can* overcome."

Mark went on to reference an encounter with Dr. Muro when he asked, physician to physician, if Conor could get better. Only later would Mark share the real content of their conversation: Dr. Muro stated that Conor's brain injury was the most severe he'd seen in his professional career. Regardless, Mark's takeaway for my sister was a positive one. He heard the desperation in her voice, and offered a lifeline.

"Kath," he said, "Conor can heal."

The greatest encouragement on this trying day came from Gerry and his family's visit to Chicago. Weary and battered in the aftermath of the RIC reality check, Gerry infused his own version of hope into Kathy's shaky confidence over a pizza dinner. His recurrent examples of integrity in how to navigate our family's unimaginable hardships over years provided reassurance. He reminded Kathy that she was stronger than she believed, and could endure the unknown challenges ahead with the same kind of endurance our mom embodied. There is something to be said about big brother support. Those opportunities Kathy had to rest her heavy heart on Gerry's broad shoulders were priceless, and fueled my sister's depleted soul with strength.

Perhaps my mom was orchestrating this journey in a piecemeal way for my sister. If the Crippens had any idea how long or arduous rehabilitation from TBI would be in those early days in the SICU, there was no way the intensity of their hope would have been as pointed or as durable. They say God gives you only as much as you can handle, but I was convinced my mom was sitting to the right of God's side, providing methodical and measured revelations to Kathy and Phil so they could remain above the choppy waters of survival. Otherwise, the grander story of TBI recovery was too big. Denial was necessary at this point. Resignation to any possibility other than Conor's full recovery was not an option.

•   •   •   •   •

During Conor's tenure as a patient in the SICU, Kathy and Phil came to know others whose stories of unexpected trauma stripped them of ordinary life. The open area of the unit corridors offered the opportunity to step out for some deep breaths. Tears flushed by worry, or relief following good news were best expressed in the common hallway. There, private stories found friendship. Some families rested in hope while others lost their fight to overcome calamity. Too often, the Crippens embraced those who openly mourned and walked through the SICU doors one last time, alone.

April 13, 2013, PRFC

As Conor prepares to move to RIC to begin his journey to full recovery, it will be a moment to mark as the Crippens leave the Advocate Illinois Masonic SICU. How can you articulate such abundance when your son is senselessly injured in a life-threatening way? How can you begin to express gratitude to trauma physicians, nurses, trauma liaisons, gentle-hearted hospital housekeepers, respiratory therapists, a phenomenal neurosurgeon, and fellow SICU family members trudging through their own pain? Collectively, everyone who met us in this journey gave hope. I personally recall the woman at the reception desk. She met us every morning with beauty, asking how everything was going, and gave us our visitor pass with a smile that somehow restored faith in the day even when we weren't quite so sure. My son and I were talking tonight about how this experience is where truly the "rubber meets the road" in life. We agreed, life is good. Although Conor's accident is still something we would have never welcomed, he is profoundly in the center of energy that includes a very strong family, open-heartedness that can seek hope, and a faith that is as sure and strong as the sun. In this regard, life is good, and helps to ensure that his road will lead to full recovery.

During the afternoon of April 15, 2013, I sat alone with Conor beside his RIC bed so my sister could have some time to take a shower or grab a cup of hot tea. I glanced at the muted TV mounted above the visitor chair in Conor's room.

"Breaking news" scrolled along the bottom of the CNN station. On the screen, I saw people in hysterics, smoke filling the scene, and pandemonium in action at the site of the Boston Marathon. Two bombs went off near the finish line as runners prepared to soak in the glow of triumph, and supporters prepared to greet them with congratulations. I watched as those with blood-drenched faces cried, searching for loved ones amidst the obstruction of smoke.

The iconic marathon race was supposed to be a day of accomplishment as thousands crossed the finish line, having endured the 26.2-mile journey toward victory. The parallel of life being heinously altered in an instant felt tangible as I looked at Conor. Another senseless and random act of violence altered the innocent lives of hundreds. I thought of the strength of the runners' legs and the endurance of their stamina. Having almost reached the finish line, their triumph turned to tragedy in an instant. Many were permanently marred by an act of hate. Conor's life, too, was altered by a random act. In an instant, he was sentenced to an all-encompassing mission to heal, just like so many in Boston that morning. His skull sat tucked beneath his abdominal fold simply because he was crossing the street. Others lost limbs because of their quest to fulfill a dream. I placed my hand on Conor's arm, again grateful that he was even here and owned a chance at life. I offered intentional prayer for those suffering in Boston. I knew Conor, too, would have been heartbroken by their devastation. We certainly did not own the patent on pain.

Winding down Conor's final days in the SICU came with a pause for relief. Blood values and vital signs were still monitored, but we were able to breathe without worry. Kathy continued to admittedly remain in the bubble, aware that the safety of Conor's SICU room would be traded for a much larger challenge and risk.

The comprehensive sendoff from the SICU was grand. One by one, the nurses, therapists, social workers, and physicians who provided miraculous care came to Conor's room offering hugs of encouragement. Kathy promised them Conor would return to thank them himself. Fr. Patrick came and said Mass at Conor's bedside. The final days with this adopted family of caregivers felt like a celebration grounded in gratitude. The ability of each SICU caregiver to save Conor's life and shepherd Kathy and Phil though this most trying life event left a permanent imprint of gratitude. We were grateful beyond words.

April 17, 2013 PRFC

We sit waiting for transfer to RIC. The monitor which connected us to Conor's medical status is now off. The EKG leads hang unused on the hook by his bed. His bed is actually unoccupied as he sits in his chair watching the construction outside his window. Conor is quite awake this morning as if he knows he is moving on down the road to literal recovery. We are celebrating this morning. Lots of smiles shared with the staff we call family; promises to come back when Conor can walk through these doors, and gifts of appreciation have all been given. The staff of SICU all signed a bed sheet with great wishes for Conor. Fr. Yaroslav (the hospital chaplain) gave to Conor his personal rosary and prayer book. We are again overwhelmed and feel like our hearts have been stretched with the love and hope for Conor from so many. Such a flood of goodness we have received over and over again. We are humbled, and my sister was literally on her knees as she shared with Conor this outpouring. It has been quite evident how interwoven all components of this experience have been. There are just too many indications that God continues to be quite busy, as Fr. Patrick repeatedly says. The Spirit has been connecting for us, showing us the way and providing comfort in so many ways as we move forward.

We have been forced by our despair to pay attention and seek God's grace in everything since Conor's accident. And we have been recipients of the grandness of love's power. My sister says over and over again she will tell Conor every story of care from those who were here and those from afar. We have had quite the lesson in faith, hope, and love, and we are just beginning. We will continue to live in awareness. Next stop: RIC. GO CONOR GO!!

The Alchemist, by Paulo Coelho, sat on Conor's beside table; a gift from a loving friend. Anticipating his transfer to the RIC, my sister began reading the book aloud to him. In the 10th Anniversary edition, the author writes in his preface,

"We all need to be aware of our personal calling. What is a personal calling? It is God's blessing, it is the path that God chose for you here on earth."

The calling of those who saved Conor's life, and those who kept my sister's spirit lifted, was indeed God's blessing, and our gratitude would remain always.

It was good that this initial chapter was so deeply rooted in grace. As we moved on to rehabilitation, God's presence was not always so tangible.

the journey towards home

☙ chapter 15 ❧

Chicago

I exited the elevator and entered the 10th floor of the Rehabilitation Institute of Chicago. I felt my insides quiver with nervous anticipation as I waited for Kathy and Conor to arrive by ambulance from the Illinois Masonic SICU. Phil was again driving from Dayton, so I planned to remain until his arrival. Phil and I didn't see one other much these days, but we would inevitably call one another, somewhere between Indianapolis and Gary, Indiana—along I-65—with "report."

I anticipated some stress from the cross-town journey, but upon Kathy and Conor's arrival through the 10th-floor elevator doors, I could see my sister's tightened face and attentiveness to Conor. Her demeanor was evidence that the ride was distressing. This was the first time since the accident that Conor rode in a vehicle, and his brain's inability to navigate changes in equilibrium caused him to vomit through most of the trip. Kathy's anxieties took their toll. Her cautious optimism upon departure from Advocate Illinois Masonic had dissipated. We remained in the reception area for what seemed like an eternity as Conor's paperwork, transfer orders, and insurance information were logged. As the unit clerk processed Conor's admission with tedious attention, I could sense my sister becoming less and less patient. Conor seemed agitated and restless beneath the stretcher restraints, and I stood by powerless as I saw my sister try to stifle her frustrations. My heart ached in new places, but I could only stand by helpless in my inability to fix.

Once the paperwork was complete, Conor was wheeled to his room. The orderly, a middle-aged man with grand stature, introduced himself as Mike. He immediately took charge by changing Conor out of his hospital gown; a symbolic gesture for sure. He placed Conor gently into bed for a much-needed rest. Over time, Mike became like family. His tenderness in speaking encouraging words to Conor would leave a gentle imprint in Kathy's heart over the weeks to come. This day, however, "Big Mike's" initial act of replacing Conor's SICU hospital gown with basketball shorts and a t-shirt from home represented a permanency that felt like a gut punch. Kathy looked around the room; it was quiet and stark. She looked at me, searching for some direction. *What happens now?*

The windows of Conor's room overlooked Lake Michigan. This view from above gave perspective that there was more to the world than Conor's condition. Spring teased the stubborn Chicago winter, and we delighted from above as bikers and boaters below reminded us that life was normal for some. Kathy looked at the sailboats on the lake and spoke of Conor's love for the water, a painful reminder of how his life had so dramatically changed.

The transition from the Advocate SICU to the RIC was tough. Stripped of constant attention and distracting monitors, the reality of Conor's condition felt heavier than even the initial days following his accident. The RIC offered various support groups and encouraged Kathy to connect with others who shared similar experiences. But my sister was reluctant to participate, feeling that if she remained separate from others who'd experienced the world of TBI, she could avoid being one of them. Surrounded by other patients who exhibited obvious deficits due to injury, Kathy still held on to her denial—her son wasn't like all the other patients—and in those first weeks, she remained rather isolated. The rules of TBI didn't yet fully apply to her Conor. Her energies were laser-focused on self-preservation.

For those who wait for their brain-injured loved ones to "wake up," time is measured by the ability to exercise a new definition of patience. There's nothing quick about brain rehabilitation. Miracles happen in the form of a drip, drip, drip over the course of repetitive therapeutic sessions. Family members sit by in support. Despite disclaimers, Kathy was one of them. Like them, her shrunken world extended no further than the RIC 10th-floor elevator doors.

Verbalizing words of hope through PRFC felt hollow as Conor continued to lay lost to injury. It had been a month since he was hit by a car. His blue helmet protected his head while his skull flaps remained sewn into his lower abdomen. His tracheostomy was plugged which meant he was breathing on his own. That was a good thing and offered proof of how far he had come, but he was still essentially unresponsive. Futile attempts to coerce reactions to close ended questions left a longing that, at times, felt bleak.

"Conor, can you give me a-thumbs up?"

"Conor, can you give your mom a hug?"

"Conor, can you give me a fist-bump?"

Such questions disappeared in the heavy silences of Conor's demeanor. His head still hung listlessly. He had no muscle strength in his neck. When out of bed, he was secured in a reclining wheel chair. He was not yet able to walk, sit up, talk, eat, or engage with others. Therapists did their initial assessments with little response from Conor. Suddenly that unyielding belief that Conor would fully recover felt precarious. I saw the uncompromising certainty of Kathy's resolve whither. These days felt long and protracted, defined by therapy sessions which felt barren. We all walked a fine line, but Kathy fought all temptation to fall from the realm of hope. Without fail, she chose to have confidence that all tomorrows would hold more possibilities than any today. She owed Conor unyielding belief that he could overcome.

Loyola continued to provide incredible support, including an opportunity for free housing. A few blocks from the RIC was Loyola's downtown Chicago campus. Fr. Patrick did a bit of finagling, and the Crippens were offered an apartment in a nearby dorm, within walking distance to the RIC. The proximity provided a multitude of perks. Family members had a place to stay, and the easing of financial worry for extended housing was literally priceless. Perhaps most beneficial for Kathy was the opportunity for a walk at the beginning and end of each day. Mornings allowed her to set her footing, to ground herself in impenetrable determination, and to be restored by the unsuspecting life of downtown Chicago. Kathy's evening walk, after Conor was tucked into bed, afforded a chance to renew in the promise that each dusk would lead to a better tomorrow.

Phil and I continued to tag-team our Chicago visits. Kathy admittedly remained in the bubble. She hadn't left Conor's side since arriving in Chicago, and her world was defined by the results of therapy sessions and tube feeding schedules. Phil, too, lived within new parameters, trying to preserve some sense of normalcy for Jack, maintain his job, and balance the fact that the rest of their world needed to turn. I witnessed Phil manage the plethora of challenges, reminded of his vast capacity to care for those he loved. Phil wasn't suddenly remarkable. I knew that long before Conor's accident. Just as Kathy's entire life prepared her ability to craft the best chance for Conor's recovery, Phil's selfless nature meant he would be anywhere, anytime to help his family plow through this unforeseen situation. Make no mistake, though: the Crippens were not alone. Hundreds, through their outreach, offered constant lifelines of hope.

When I was in Chicago, Kathy and I had a routine. I was respectful of her need for solitude especially at the beginning of each day. I left the dorm first, giving her the opportunity to reset herself. I made my way to a nearby Einstein Bagel and ordered coffee for myself and a hot tea and buttered bagel to-go for her. I then sat down at a window seat with clear vision to the Loyola dorm. I sipped my coffee, waiting for Kathy to exit the revolving doors. I still wasn't used to nor did I like the fact she was so alone in her burden. I watched her make her way down the sidewalk, blending her step with others journeying toward their day. Her gait betrayed her yoke. I still couldn't believe—even after all these weeks—that life brought her to this point. Love for Conor gave no other choice than to renew herself each morning in hope that this day would offer even slight improvement. With her scarf wrapped around her neck and her "Believe"-embroidered satchel hoisted on her shoulder, she set off yearning for therapy sessions to confirm progress. I, too, had to reset the renewed brokenness of my heart.

Each morning, Kathy greeted Conor with delight and purpose. I helped her get him out of bed, dress him in his signature shorts and t-shirt, and sit him in his wheelchair. Positioning him near the expansive window, Kathy would then pull up a chair and sit beside him. She described the weather and talked about the sailboats on the lake and the bikers on Lakeshore Drive. Proximity to the lake was one of the reasons Conor loved Loyola. Kathy hoped the descriptive scene just beyond the window would jumpstart something, anything. She told him about the day ahead and the updates from home. She read from *The Alchemist*, and Dr. Seuss' *Oh, the Places You'll Go*, inspiring her son to seek his way toward awareness. She read letters from family and friends that arrived daily, offering constant encouragement. She hugged him, hoping to ignite response.

One day, shortly after Conor arrived at the RIC, the middle-aged nursing assistant who cared for Conor shared with us the loss of her 18-year-old son due to a gunshot wound. The randomness of his death and the palpability of her grief were evident. Once we knew of her suffering, her lackluster demeanor made sense. She carried her grief in her face, betrayed by saddened eyes. Her shoulders hung, heavy from the grief of his passing. She told us the 5-year anniversary of her son's death was approaching, and voiced bittersweet gratitude that Conor had been given a chance at life. She expressed hope that God would heal him fully. One day, she said with envious longing, Conor would be able to tell the stories of how the angels comforted him during these days of silence.

Kathy and I were humbled. Grace was spoken through this woman's personal grief; a reminder to keep our eyes focused and ears open to the whispers of inspiration. She lifted us out of our story and gave the much-needed perspective that so many other people lost loved ones to random accidents. As Conor worked so hard in therapy, we, too, were called to work hard to remain grateful for his life. There would be no limits placed on the hope that each tomorrow would continue to be a bit better than today. Our gift was right before us.

Kathy and I talked about the needed reminders to remain in faith. Even so, despite my sister's awareness of the tangibility of

God's touch, it was never enough. She was needy of reassurance. Continued progress in healing to full recovery was a guarantee she desperately wanted.

The RIC is in the business of research and clinical practice based on evidence. Dr. David Ripley, the Medical Director for Brain Injury and Rehabilitation, and his medical team entourage rounded with their patients each morning, assessing changes or improvements and addressing any concerns. Driven by the mission of cutting edge research objectives, the team approach was to design a plan for each day. Science met hope on the RIC 10th floor, but expectation following a traumatic brain injury is like watching dough rise; only lapses of time confirm progress. Dr. Ripley's initial plan of care with Conor was the introduction of various medications designed to stimulate the brain, hoping to jumpstart the long road toward higher brain function. Dr. Ripley tweaked Conor's medications based on his daily assessments. It was a game of trial and error to see what worked and what didn't. He reminded us from the first days at RIC that the brain heals from the inside out. It would take time. Considering Conor's severe and encompassing brain trauma, the restoration of brain function would be laborious and painstaking.

Physical, occupational and speech therapists dedicated to making a difference dripped with creativity as they tried new therapeutic models. They collaborated with one another in hopes that somehow, they could find a key to unlock some part of Conor's functionality. Day after day we watched as Conor's wheelchair was pushed up to the stationary bike, his shoes strapped to its pedals. Riding a bike, after all, is something never forgotten, right? The automated pedaling encouraged muscle recall, and for days, the machine passively rotated Conor's legs as if they were propelling, but they weren't. Day after day I stood behind Conor as Kathy sat next to him. She cheered him on, she encouraged him, and when his legs seemed lethargic, she pressed on his feet, willing them to remember.

And then one day, the monitor blinked. It was fleeting. *Did we just see a green light?* But then Joe, Conor's physical therapist, started nodding his head. Yes, this was a breakthrough. Blinking green lights meant Conor was initiating movement. YES, we all said again. And then the next time, we saw a few more blinking green lights. Conor was lighting up. This was the slow but triumphant journey through brain injury.

Drawing with a marker on a white board, holding a spoon on command, throwing a plastic ball into a basket, and the ability to pick up a toothpaste cap were all small victories that came over weeks of therapeutic sessions. The first time Conor turned his thumb upward on request felt like we'd just witnessed a moon landing. We observed the beginnings of rebirth, resting in the minimal accomplishments of each day. At a snail's pace, Conor's movements were transitioning from passive to purposeful. As we cheered Conor through each therapy session, the reminder was constant: through brokenness, new life flows. We were not the only ones invited to travel the unexpected road, and not every day yielded success. The call was to remain vigilant.

In the days following Conor's admission to the RIC, the medical and therapeutic team met with Kathy and Bridget to give their initial assessment and therapy goals, and to discuss the long-term planning regarding his continued rehabilitation. The clinical assessment, although no surprise, was still difficult to hear: Conor's brain injury was severe. His CT scan showed significant damage, and scattered throughout his brain were indications of diffuse shearing, or tearing of brain fibers. His entire brain had been affected. His recovery, they reminded, would take more than months. It was even suggested that Conor may never be capable of being by himself, because he will never again possess high-level ability to function independently.

You will never be able to leave him home alone, my sister was told. *He won't know what to do if the house catches on fire.*

The words pierced their hopeful hearts, and the conference left them swarming in fractured yearnings.

Despair threatened the room, but Kathy was determined to do right by Conor. As Bridget was overcome with tears, Kathy remained measured and calm. After hearing reality-based prognoses, Kathy pulled up iPad videos of Conor in his "come from behind" run in the year's prior Ohio state high school semi-final track meet. He didn't win that race, but there in recorded motion, was his drive. Conor exemplified unyielding spirit. It was still in him, Kathy told those in white coats sitting around the conference table. Clinicians are called upon to deliver the facts, not give false hope. This day they did their job, but so did Kathy and Bridget. Their charge was to communicate the healing promise of Conor, whose ability to overcome and restore was, for them, a given.

Following the reality check of the clinical team's assessment, Kathy returned to Conor's room to find him surrounded by those he loved the most. Balancing the harsh realities of the painstaking recovery was a constant flow of visitors. Friends from home, relatives from Chicago, and once-strangers—now prayer partners through Conor's Facebook page—offered revitalizing energy and encouragement. Kathy fought the urge to protect Conor by keeping others from seeing him, but she also knew the company of those who knew him was therapeutic. She knew somewhere inside Conor's unresponsiveness was the ability to know and experience his friends' support. And they came. Conor's room became the meeting place for all who believed in his capacity to heal. We called it love therapy.

Conor, without his helmet, was lying in his bed. Without his cranial bone flaps, the shape of his head was concave. Bridget sat on one side, Holly, my youngest daughter sat on the other. These three cousins shared friendship reaching far beyond familial connection. They grew up together, often confused as to whose kitchen table they belonged to more. Toddler memories of shared bathtub splashing and experiments with scissors to cut one another's wisps of angel-soft hair yielded unique closeness. Holly was more sister than cousin, and her presence for Conor and especially Bridget was immeasurable.

Also present this day were Keenan and Casey. They were listening to an iPod playlist that Conor created prior to his accident. Laughter and the beat of rap music filled the room, and for the first time, Conor was giving fist-bumps in the midst of their shared fun. The scene before Kathy spoke louder than all medical team projections. This was love's healing power. These were the people Conor knew, who believed in him and the extraordinary spirit that he brought to this challenge. Conor's peers declared more authority than those in the conference room down the 10th floor hall in the form of a fist bump. This was where hope was restored. The scene reminded Kathy and Bridget that Conor would continue to lead the way. As long as we kept our hearts connected with his, if we followed his example of perseverance, he would bring us along to witness his journey of healing.

Shortly thereafter, Conor began to perform more simple movements on command. Asking him to toss a small rubber ball, raise his head on command or meet his friends with a raised arm were all indications that physical headways were sluggishly re-emerging. His abilities to be conscious or aware, however, were much harder to assess. He still wasn't verbally communicating, so we rested with his ability to occasionally instigate intentional movements.

Protection of Conor's head was a priority. His skull flaps were still embedded in his abdomen, and although he wore his helmet while out of bed, nighttime left the safety of his healing brain vulnerable. The thought of Conor falling out of bed or inadvertently bumping his head without skull protection was inconceivable. Conor wasn't the first RIC patient to have skull bones removed, so the plan of care for such patients was standard. A safety net encased the bed frame so that further injury to the brain was minimized. Each night, after putting Conor to bed, Kathy would zip the netted enclosure. The visual of him lying in a fetal position caged within the mesh protector is difficult even now to remember. It may have been standard care on the 10th floor, but for us, it felt amiss. Every night was a painful reminder of the reality of his condition.

⟿ chapter 16 ⟿

April 27, 2013 would have been Neil's 58th birthday. His absence in Conor's story was profound. During these early days of Conor's recovery, I missed Neil and was angry with him all at the same time. He would have been in contact with my sister daily, wanting to know the update on Conor and offering his unique brand of support. Although I tried to retain a gentle and accepting heart in the aftermath of his suicide, I was angry he wasn't there for Kathy when she needed him most.

Neil loved to attend Conor's track meets. He loved watching Conor, with his head back, chest forward, running with the gait like a gazelle. After his first suicide attempt, Neil spent quite a bit of time with Kathy's boys. He loved to probe Conor on his post high school dreams, encourage him to "see the world," and insist that next time Conor ran a race, he could break his own record. Neil liked to encourage, and would push his young nieces and nephews to strive for greater things. He would have been more than vested in Conor's recovery.

Kathy and I talked about how this mission of Conor's recovery could have helped Neil save himself. Surely, he would've known his role of uncle and brother was needed more now than ever; the gift of him, albeit like the wind, would have added a pivotal dimension of support for Kathy. They would have saved one another, if given the chance. So many days when I sat by my sister, feeling futile in my ability to make things better for her, I imagined Neil unexpectedly walking through the door, bringing his dynamic breeze of refreshment. He would have hugged Kathy and undoubtedly made her laugh with lighthearted reminders of our family brand of humor.

One of Neil's iconic stories happened when Pat, age 16, was in the intensive care unit because his esophagus had been obliterated by the voluntary ingestion of drain cleaner. I was nine years old at the time and have little recollection which is, in itself, a bit peculiar. I've since learned that family trials are best handled when light is shed and imperfection is embraced. Unfortunately, at that time, the Grogan dynamic was stuck in shame. My mom was overcome with heartache and confusion regarding her oldest child's mystifying act. Her bewilderment left her in shock, perhaps crippling her ability to cope. This time, the one to catch the overflow was Neil.

Pat was dependent on a ventilator to breathe. Like Conor, his tube-connected appearance in the hospital was in stark contrast to the vibrant young man we were more familiar with. Unlike Conor, Pat was lucid and aware, despite life support. Neil, aged 14, came to see Pat. Barely old enough to be a visitor in the intensive care unit, Neil showed up with a mission; stretching his brother's fall from grace beyond shame to the disarming realm of laughter. Yes, it was a Band-Aid, but for Neil, Band-Aids were a default.

Neil started his comedic monologue poking fun at the hospital scene in which Pat was the center. Teasing with Pat and making lighthearted observations eased Pat's anxiety. You could see it in his eyes and in the way his body shook from silent laughter. The presentation ended with a line that would linger as a source of humor long after Pat was discharged.

"Trachs are for kids," Neil said in reference to the tracheostomy breathing tube.

Defusing the critical graveness of Pat's condition with silliness was the best medicine of all. The inside family joke would stick, and so would Neil's ability to save the day.

What Pat didn't know at the time was that, upon exiting the hospital room, Neil leaned against the hallway wall. A pall of gray overcame his face, and his legs buckled in diminished strength. The call to uplift took its toll. Neil knew he needed to provide some relief for Pat, and he did just that, but the cost was evident. It was as if Neil gave to Pat all that he had, which left him depleted of emotional energy. Over the remainder of his life, Neil showed up—providing similar lifelines—and just as quickly, he left. I think during his fleeting and not-frequent-enough visits home, Neil gave us all he had. Exiting was the only way he could restore himself.

Now that Kathy was in the midst of such an intense call to bravery, I imagined Neil popping up in Chicago, sitting through a physical therapy session and coaching Conor to pedal faster on the stationary bike, throw the ball farther, or stand unsupported longer. He would have put his arm around my sister and made some observation that allowed the therapeutic flow of laughter to lighten her burden. I missed him terribly.

As May came, so did the anticipation for the Kentucky Derby. Historically, this was a notable day for our family. Leading up to the iconic horse race, we engaged in group texts and phone calls sharing with one another the name of the horse we picked to win. The selection process was quite sophisticated for most of us; usually it was based on the horse's name. If the horse or jockey had a name laced with any indication of Irish heritage, inevitably that was the popular pick for winning horse. The only family member to take seriously a methodical and quantitative horse choice was Gerry. So, it was no surprise that he drove to Chicago to watch the race with Conor and then returned home to Ohio the same day. Gerry did things like that. Same-day trips to Chicago to offer Kathy his brand of support were timely. He seemed to know when Kathy needed him most, and in the aftermath of Neil's absence, Gerry carried the torch of brotherhood. His reminders to Kathy that she mirrored our mother's capacity to love when life was hard left an imprint. Gerry's brand of support that day embodied the commitment to our mom's request. *Always take care of one other.* I couldn't tell you which horse won that Derby day, but I remember Gerry showing up. He always did, and still does.

While in Chicago, I could envelop myself in the same vacuum of hope my sister demanded. Being with Conor made it easy to remain positive and believe without doubt his capacity to recover. When you were with him, his essence transcended the sheared brain fibers. We knew Conor was in there, and he just needed time and manicured attention to come back in full force. For anyone to think otherwise was just not acceptable. The expansive conversations we were having with our friends and prayer warriors offered constant reassurance that faith in God's possibility and trust in Conor's therapists could lead to his restoration. I especially needed to keep my head above the doubt pool so that I could provide a constant supply of hopeful oxygen for my sister, particularly on those long and lonely days when we wondered when progress would show up. I knew it was my job to remain absolute in my conviction: my sister needed me to be a stalwart reminder of confidence in believing that healing was endless for Conor.

I had no trouble maintaining my protective armor of conviction. That is, until I went home—which wasn't very often. Mark and I had little time to talk extensively regarding Conor's condition, his therapy regime, and the state of my sister's existence. He had a more difficult time believing Conor could recover from this catastrophic brain injury, and I knew it was easier to believe in Conor's capacity to heal when you were with him. Whereas Kathy and Phil were on a learning curve regarding TBI, Mark knew how debilitated Conor really was. Compounding his fear was his unique and close relationship with Conor, whom Mark often referred to as his third son. Their mutual love of our lake house, their propensity to enjoy discussions of philosophy and theology, and their delight in eating bone-in filet of beef steaks—rare—was the stuff of their relationship. Conor's catastrophic accident left Mark fragmented, torn by his deep affection for his son-like nephew. The reality was that none of us knew for certain whether Conor would ever navigate his way back from this profoundly compromised state.

I was with Kathy more than I was home. Mark was often left by himself, drowning in fear that this young man he loved so much would never regain wholeness. In some ways, I chose the best of me for my sister, and justified the distance from my husband. Ultimately, I knew on some level that Mark and I could handle the stress because our 40 years of tenured commitment meant something. I banked on that guarantee as I drove off again and again toward my sister in Chicago. This accident propelled Mark and me into unchartered territory where we didn't know how to rise above our own apprehensions. Honesty with each other had become illusive. The longing for Conor to be okay thwarted our ability to love each other with understanding. It would be a long summer for Mark and me, as the silences of our unspoken worries created a chasm between us. The stakes to our self-preservation were too high; it was easier just not to talk about it. While I chose to land on the side of belief that Conor could overcome, Mark couldn't help but continue to prepare himself emotionally and intellectually that the odds were not in Conor's favor. His perception that I was enabling my sister's inability to be realistic conflicted with my refusal to entertain even an iota of agreement. The fact is, my sister needed me to be stronger than her weakest doubts. There was no way I could fake certainty with her. My promise to be with her in any way she needed was absolute.

In hindsight, I regret I didn't offer Mark more of a safe place to express his fears and sadness. Whereas Kathy and I were able reinforce the choice to hope by mutual empowerment, Mark had no one to verbalize his fears with, not even me. Even if I validated his sentiments, I felt as if I was betraying my sister's unspoken trust to remain absolute in my creed that Conor could overcome. No cracks allowed.

Coming home offered the opportunity for me to be restored by the blessing of Conor's local community of supporters. It seemed everywhere I went—in the grocery store, to the gym, or to my work—someone would stop me and ask how he was doing. Conor's story remained on the radar of so many due to the Facebook page. I found myself posting updates as a way to provide "in-the-moment" inspiration for Kathy. The sustained response provided opportunities for her to be elevated from the drowning despair that all too often loomed, especially when Conor's therapy sessions left her wanting more. The cyber dialogue offered her a conduit to the world of belief and hope. I witnessed the encouraging power of others in their responses and the tangible outpouring that resulted from the social media connection.

Bridget, too, found comfort in those around her. As she navigated her last weeks of college, Xavier University students came together and organized a fundraiser for Conor's family, raising several hundred dollars. She wrote:

April 28, 2013 PRFC

I was almost speechless when…I thought about all the college students who gave a couple of dollars out of their own pocket, and how it added up to the money that will help to heal my brother…Once again, I am humbled and overwhelmed by the amount of love and goodness of people. This experience has been awful, and at some points unbearable for my family and I…. However, the goodness of people and the support we have been given has literally carried us through this time and has reminded us of the remaining plans life has for my brother. For me, as an almost graduate of Xavier, I have never been prouder to call myself a Xavier Musketeer, and I have never been so proud to share the last four years of my life with such genuinely good people.

The students and faculty of Alter High School sent care packages filled with relics, reminding us to remain in the realm of faith. Kathy received packages from the school filled with teacher encouragement and student letters. Souvenirs representative of very personal experiences where shared, giving testimony that triumph happens despite heartache. Religious medals, homemade bracelets, and charms fortified by hope were worn every day by my sister. Homespun art and framed words of inspiration hung by Conor's bedside. Hundreds of creative "GO CONOR GO!" signs were copied and taped all along the walls of Conor's room providing tangible outreach of the wide community prayer group. The hope of life beyond the 10th floor windows was framed by the proof of uplifting support.

These interactions were all reminders that God's range went far beyond my previous understanding of grace, and deepened my trust that all of us who loved Conor were indeed being carried.

Bridget's graduation from Xavier University was scheduled for early May. Kathy was reluctant to leave Conor, but she knew she needed to attend the celebration not only for Bridget, but also for herself. Kathy remained in Chicago since March 17, and the exercise of stepping outside the bubble was something she knew she needed to do at some point. Attending a celebration of accomplishment for Bridget was a venture she could justify. There was only one condition: she would fly in and out of Cincinnati, where Xavier is located. She insisted she would not go home again to Dayton until Conor was with her. Mark and I offered to stay in Chicago for the weekend.

The night before she left for Ohio, Mark asked Kathy how she was tending to herself in the midst of everything. She was taken aback by the question. Upon reflection, though, she realized that her self-care came from her ability to be present to God's care. By remaining open to look and listen carefully, grace would ultimately support her need for guidance grounded in hope. She recalled Conor's own words that he wrote in "Yahweh's Symphony," which gave voice to the way God touches our lives. Now, with the thousands of prayer warriors connected through Facebook, the work of the therapists, and the strength of Conor, the symphonic melodies were fully connected. Conor knew the possibility of God's touch all along, and my sister was in full-throttle belief because of the inspiration of her son's words. She was being supported by Yahweh's Symphony.

chapter 17

We were relieved and thrilled when surgery was scheduled to replace Conor's skull flaps. Simultaneously, we felt a shift in Conor. He was more awake and able to follow more of the simple commands, and he delighted us with his ability to toss a ball. One of the RIC doctors offered encouragement by explaining that, when the cranial bones are returned to their rightful place, the restoration of more normal barometric pressure within the skull offers the brain a more natural environment. Hence, the potential for healing increases. Our faith was renewed even more. Restoring Conor's head to physical wholeness, we trusted, would only accelerate his healing.

Fr. Patrick and Sr. Jean were intuitive in showing up when Kathy needed a booster shot of faith. The day before Conor's surgery, they came to his RIC room to celebrate Mass; their companionship felt like a warm embrace. Fr. Patrick talked about the tenderness of God's spirit. His words encouraged the palpability of grace. My sister listened as her advocate of faith reassured her that God was sure and constant. Sr. Jean reminded us that Conor's surgery day was the feast day of Our Lady of Fatima. Any infusion of Mary into our faith quest was welcome, as we chose to believe her mother's love could lead Conor toward his new phase of healing.

Re-entering the corridors of Illinois Masonic for Conor's "flap-back" surgery was unexpectedly difficult. The post-traumatic wave of heaviness took Kathy by surprise. The truncated recall of the accident and immediate aftermath conjured a reopening of her deepest wound: the fact that this accident even happened at all. The anticipation of Conor's skull restoration included relief until she walked back into the SICU. Entering through the familiar automatic doors suddenly felt even more onerous. The silver lining, however, was the opportunity to reunite with the doctors and nurses who saved Conor's life in the first place. Dr. Muro was encouraged by Conor's healing, and those who cared so diligently in Conor's initial fight for life were thrilled to see him on the road to recovery.

That Tuesday morning, our surgical waiting room experience felt quite different than the lonely Sunday afternoon eight weeks earlier when Conor's skull was dismantled. Now, most chairs were filled with people sipping coffee, making small talk, or flipping through magazines offering springtime salad recipes. The elderly Betty White-type hospital volunteer managed communication between surgical teams and waiting family members with the voice and smile of a loving grandmother. The collective accompaniment made Conor's surgery seem less critical. Plus, we knew Dr. Muro was in charge, providing even more reassurance.

We were told the surgery would take several hours, so we chose to grab a bite to eat at a nearby deli. Stepping outside the chill of the hospital, we were met with another encouraging cloudless sky. The sun warmed the hospital chill. We peeled our sweaters off, feeling the freedom offered by deep breaths of fresh air. We couldn't help but be nourished by the unfiltered radiance, choosing again to receive the blessing as a sign of hope for Conor. Indeed, we were not disappointed by nature's warm embrace. The surgery was another success. Dr. Muro reported an uncomplicated and expected outcome. Hundreds of titanium staples circled each side of Conor's newly shaven head, securing his bone flaps back in their rightful place.

Over the next few days, Conor's head and face swelled. Discoloration and bruising, although expected, were difficult to see. Imagining how sore and painful it must have felt made our hearts weep again for Conor, who'd already endured so much. Once again, we were sentenced to patience as we kept a bedside vigil. Our minds knew his swollen-shut eyes would open brightly again, and the question-mark-shaped incisions would be concealed by a vibrant regrowth of his ginger-colored hair. But still our hearts ached.

Conor returned to the RIC four days following surgery. The blue protective helmet was tucked with Conor's belongings, having served its purpose. Now it was time to get back to the hard work of therapy. There were times when we felt Conor return to life, but they were random and unexpected. It was difficult to watch therapists ask Conor to respond to new challenges; often he didn't. The hope that his "flap-back" surgery would result in accelerated progress remained unrealized. The Crippens fought discouragement. The therapists were charged, again, with finding some way to reach Conor's mind despite his diffuse damage. Not every therapy session yielded "success" or "improvement" for us who wanted nothing more than to have Conor whole again. We sat observing as novices with no other choice than to trust in the therapists' ability to lay groundwork for tangible progress.

Our appreciation of the therapists grew with each session. Their methods were intended to connect one muscle memory to another. Speech therapists worked on swallowing exercises which help the tongue remember how to push food back toward the throat and ultimately help Conor speak again. Occupational therapists worked with fine motor exercises so that the brain could recall how to move hands and fingers with purpose.

The stream of progress was slow. First, there was the day that Conor was able to stand, partially supported by his own leg strength. We held our breaths in awe. Then, he did it again. Joe, Conor's physical therapist, then harnessed him to a treadmill, and manually moved his feet to meet the moving track. We were thrilled in seeing his endurance and consistency of leg move-ment, indicating some rebirth somewhere in his healing brain. And then Conor swallowed for the first time; a tiny spoonful of applesauce. And then another day, he was transferred from bed to chair—once requiring two people—with arm support only. The encouragement we banked on these good days had to be enough of a deposit to last on other days when the promising intent of therapy sessions left us feeling flat.

Often, Conor was sleepy, slow to respond, or just not inter-ested in the tasks presented to him. Such days confirmed the reality of how tedious and slow TBI recovery is. Every day was an exercise in remaining positive, as Conor was fighting his way back one step at a time. Kathy sat through each therapy session reminding Conor of memories she hoped would trigger a response. My admiration was great for Conor and others who needed to fight for the opportunity to relearn. The winds of opti-mism whispered softly in these days, and we had no choice but to remain hopeful as the gentle breeze propelled us all forward.

Weekends did not include the intense therapy schedule offered by weekdays, but that did not deter us from doing our own work with Conor. Visits from family and friends offered laughter therapy. We wheeled Conor through the streets of downtown Chicago, hoping some fresh air and exposure to the sun would restore his stamina. Sometimes, we even put our own physical therapy hats on. Mark, on his frequent trips to Chicago, liked to take on the role of therapist.

Mark and I may have had a hard time communicating with each other during these initial months of Conor's injury, but he had no difficulty in connecting with Conor. On a warm June afternoon, while spending the afternoon with Conor, Mark made the simple request, "How about if you sit up today, Conorman?" Prior to this day, Conor wasn't able to sit upright unsupported. Mark then took Conor's legs, dangled them off the side of the bed and supported his back, and sat next to him. Mark talked to him as he always did, reminding him of memories they shared together. There was some sort of magical connection between the two of them, because the more Mark encouraged him, the steadier Conor became. I think it was probably talk of their next steak meal that did it.

On Father's Day weekend, Mark and I suggested Kathy and Phil enjoy an evening to themselves. Since March 16, their lives had been defined exclusively by Conor's needs. Distance defined their existence, and I'm sure they had not conversed about anything unrelated to Conor's recovery in months. Mark and I felt useless in our inability to help them, so the opportunity for us to assume the role of surrogate parents for a night was a win-win for everyone.

Sunday morning, Kathy and Phil returned to the RIC after their evening together. They looked a bit more rested. The four of us sat with Conor in his room, and Phil and Mark decided it was time for another home-grown therapy session. Today, we thought, was a good day to work on Conor's ability to stand. We each assumed our role: I was in charge of bracing Conor's feet,

Kathy would be supporting from behind, and the two dads were tasked with lifting Conor to a standing position.

"One, two, three!" we all said together as Phil and Mark lifted Conor to stand. For hours that Sunday afternoon, we helped Conor help himself, a miracle that felt bold when Conor stood independently for a brief second. We cheered each time we felt Conor's leg muscles engage. The four of us surrounded him with the kind of ready arms surrounding a baby learning to stand. We cheered his accomplishment, and we gave one another high-fives in celebration. Mark and Phil left later that afternoon for their separate drives home, elated by the progress of the day. Their backs, however, told a different story. Muscle strains to help Conor stand stiffened on the five-hour drive home leaving them with a compromised ability to walk. They both indulged in a dose of Advil, a session of stretching, and a bit of vodka on ice to help ease their pain. They were left with a profound respect for physical therapists, and agreed that their back discomfort was the best Father's Day gift ever.

Conor spent 10 weeks as an inpatient at the RIC. The multi-therapeutic approach to treating brain injury was impressive. The plan was designed to help patients learn weight balance and coordination, facilitating the movement of lips and mouth to restore the ability to swallow and talk. Music therapy involved songs by Dave Matthews Band, designed to awaken Conor's love for his favorite music. Pet therapy brought dogs to his bedside in hopes of igniting the heart connection Conor had with his family's golden retrievers. Each new therapist wanted to know about Conor: his interests, his likes, and what excited him.

Throughout these arduous days, Kathy and Phil did not weaken or diminish in their belief that Conor would recover fully. Yes, through the course of many days, honesty would spill through tears, sunken postures, or sighs of exhaustion, but there was not a day when hope did not prevail as the sun set toward their tomorrow. Kathy's understanding of the extent of his recovery was deepening. This was a complicated process, but the navigation from day to day was uncomplicated. The combination of a great faith pushing doubt aside, a love that overcomes fear, and the ability to laugh about something each day propelled the journey onward. Unfaltering was the determination to remain focused as Conor worked so hard to restore himself, always surrounded by those who believed he could. Kathy drove the bus of belief, and if you didn't buy into a happy ending to this complicated and long ride, you had no business climbing on board. Daily goals were important, but Kathy and Phil were finding the journey itself was the blessing that continued to provide the ability to place one foot in front of the other. Conor's ability to talk, eat, and ultimately live an independent life were non-negotiable goals. Getting there continued to require a cocktail of positivity and full-time commitment.

A few weeks before Conor left the RIC, all five Crippens had the opportunity to spend the weekend together as family. This was the manna of all healing. Unknowingly, siblings carry a code set early in family life. Their place within a family structure translates toward the greater world. The chance to be together ignited the usual dynamic for Bridget, Conor, and Jack. Conor and Jack played thumb wars, and their brotherly competitive spirit connected the 10th-floor rehabilitation room with normalcy. Smiles communicated old understanding, eye contact opened familiarity of the soul, and Kathy could not help but be nourished by the fact that her whole family was together.

When Kathy later called me to share the joy of that day, I remember hearing a softness in her voice. I could tell this was a therapeutic day for her. The intangible benefits of being together armed her weary heart. She saw her own children offer the same sibling support that she, Gerry, and I knew quite well. It was a day that began the final turn toward home.

A few days later, Bridget wrote:

June 7, 2013 PRFC

The strength that Conor has is incredible, but he's still learning about weight balance and coordination. With Joe, the physical therapist holding one side (who we love), and my dad or Jack on the other side of him holding him up, Conor was able to walk tall and strong several times around the 10th floor. He looks better walking than he ever has before.

Conor also has been becoming a pro at swallowing and working his lips and mouth, hopefully in preparation for talking. There is nothing that is so awaited by my family than Conor talking. It's very easy to miss hearing his voice or his laugh, so we pray boldly and with faith for that voice to find its way.

As we approach the date when we can take Conor home, my family and I become more excited. His journey is still long ahead of him and will take more endurance and patience, but never before have I ever been so certain in how this journey, or as my family has come to call it, his "awakening," will end. Fr. Patrick came and had a Mass for us yesterday in Conor's room. Through the readings, he explained that sometimes we need to not look forward at the journey we still have left, but look behind us and see where we've been. To appreciate what we've already accomplished, and most importantly, what a miracle Conor has already been. He said hope is not so much its own factor in this process, but it is a byproduct of faith. This instantaneous change of life for us is not about understanding the why or how, but purely and sometimes blindly, as if we are feeling with our hands through the dark, choosing to have faith. And that is something that my family has chosen from the very beginning. All sorts of emotions come with this journey, but every day my family chooses to rest in what is good. Because of that, and because of the strength I see every day from my mom, my dad, Jack, and Conor, I've never been more proud to call myself a part of this family.

As always, this faith could not be sustained without all of your prayers, thoughts, support, and love. We are forever indebted to your kindness, more than words can express. So today we choose to pray for gratitude, for Conor's voice, and for all of you. As always, Go Conor Go!

✏ chapter 18 ✏

Centerville, Ohio

June 29, 2014

The cul-de-sac was lined with people sharing smiles and chatting with each other in anticipation. Lofty white clouds brushed the blue skies, offering a celebratory sign that the angels were dancing with joy. The heat of the day was settling in. Some June days start out uncharacteristically cool, then surrender to the rising heat of summer. This was one of them. People fanned themselves with their homemade signs reading "Welcome home Conor!" Other posters were decorated with bold-colored markers, spelling out the now-familiar cheer, "Go Conor Go!"

This was the much-anticipated day. Conor was coming home.

A 12-foot-wide paper banner stretched across the base of the Crippen driveway. "Welcome Home Crippens, GO CONOR GO" was painted with wide brush strokes in bold color. Former teachers, classmates, and friends waited. The air was hopeful, chatter born of excitement and relief that Conor was finally coming home. Jack held the leashes attached to their family's two dogs, Lucy and Sophie. Bridget and Holly skipped along the street, releasing their excited energy. Gerry wrapped his embracing arm around my shoulders. I could sense his relief. Our little sister survived months of fractured existence; each day presented a challenge to believe love was stronger than pain. Now, she too, was coming home.

The dark blue Honda CRV approached, slowing at the stop sign where Conor used to wait for the school bus as an elementary school child. Phil, driving at a parade-like pace, waved his arm out the open driver seat window, giving a thumbs-up as he entered the tunnel of people so enthused to welcome Conor. He sat in the front passenger seat wearing a baseball cap and sunglasses, reflective of ordinary time. The reality was anything but ordinary. Kathy was in the back seat with the waxy smile of a mannequin. I could read her look: humbled, scared, tentative, and relieved all at the same time. I wouldn't know until later how harrowing the car ride from Chicago had been.

The five-hour drive had taken its toll. Conor suffered several episodes of vomiting, requiring stops to clean and regroup. Not equipped yet to handle the stress on his equilibrium, motion sickness made the drive more than a bit stressful. Once off the highway, their final stop—close to home—allowed for one last change of clothes. The soiled clothes from the journey were thrown into the dumpster of the BP station just down the road.

Phil pulled into their driveway, breaking through the banner like the hometown favorite football team entering the crusade. Ben and Mark helped Conor out of the car and placed him in the rented wheelchair. He was not yet steady enough to walk independently. The Crippens appeared in the street, with onlookers cheering shouts of victory. Conor sat, his head still hung toward his chest. We weren't sure if he even knew he was home; his awareness seemingly distant and buried deep within the injury to his brain. We had not heard his voice since March.

New to their front lawn landscape was a wheelchair-accessible ramp constructed along the walkway and front door with the scent of fresh-planed wood. Larry DeRoo, a bridge engineer by trade and father of Conor's good friends, toiled for days prior to Conor's homecoming constructing a ramp that would make Conor's transport easier. Upon seeing the new landscape addition, Phil rested his face in his hands. His fatigue was overtaken by tears of gratitude.

I walked beside my sister as she navigated her way toward the crowd that had gathered around their driveway. This was the first time since the night of Conor's accident that she walked the once-ordinary blacktop of her life. Her return home marked the realization that the dream she envisioned each day while in Chicago fell short of resolution. She couldn't speak, dumbed by weariness and an overwhelming gratitude for the large number of people who showed up. These were the same people who dialogued with her daily through cyberspace, offering a lifeline in hope that this day was possible. But now they were physically before her, and it felt too much. She could offer only hugs: a morsel of what these people had given to her.

Kathy looked exhausted, but I could also see trepidation. She was lost. Since the night of Conor's accident, his care and rehabilitation were crafted within walls of safety by healthcare professionals. Daily routines were dictated by accomplished and highly educated therapists. Liquid tube feedings appeared every 8 hours from some hospital supply room. Staff physicians navigated daily tweaks to Conor's overall well-being. Now, the open air to clear the mind with a brisk walk was left behind on Michigan Avenue. Kathy and Phil were on their own. While greeting those who gathered in support, Kathy wore a smile, masking her uncertainty of how life would proceed. Once again, her demeanor begged the answer to a familiar question: *now what do we do?*

Mark and Ben flanked Conor, supporting him as he entered his home, not through the front door in a wheelchair via handicap ramp, but in the familiar way all our children come home:

through the garage. Two steps up, and with help, Conor was inside his home. I was encouraged by the shedding of Mark's "realism" upon seeing Conor return to the familiar. It seemed the paralyzing fear that defined his time away from Conor was replaced with the contagious optimism we all felt when with him.

The good news was Conor's ability to walk with assistance into his house. The challenging news, however, was that the Crippen house really wasn't designed to be handicapped accessible. Navigation through the doorways while supporting Conor, especially into the downstairs powder room, was a bit tricky. Kathy and Mark shimmied with Conor into the bathroom. Without saying words, they were thinking the same thing: *OK... here we go.*

One thing Kathy had learned regarding TBI was that rest was imperative. Brain function after trauma is especially taxing, and the fatigue can be debilitating. Following the car ride from Chicago, Conor needed some downtime. The downstairs study had been transformed: comfortable reading chairs were replaced with a hospital bed. A monitor with camera capabilities was propped so that Conor could be observed at all times while resting. An IV pole for G-tube feedings sat at the head of the bed, next to the supply of boxed nutrition. A basket with hygiene supplies, wound coverings, G-tube gauze dressings, and plastic gloves lay next to the packages of size-medium men's pull-up Depend-brand underwear. And across from Conor's new bed was a couch where Kathy, Phil, Bridget, and Jack would take turns with nighttime watch duty.

The challenge of Conor's restoration suddenly felt even more vast. The responsibility in crafting a plan for his rehabilitation now fell solely in the laps of Kathy and Phil. In this homecoming, Kathy felt like they were bringing home a newborn for the first time. No one knew what to expect. I thought I'd seen the best of my sister rise while in Chicago, but now that Conor was home, she set off on an unwavering path with one goal in mind. It was time to get to work.

Home offers the best scenario for resurgence, and Conor's return home proved that in the most dramatic way. The day after his return, he started walking independently. The marked response to the familiarity and comfort of home reminded me of my mom. Once again, we felt she was channeling her spirit through Conor.

In the last several years of my mom's life, she endured more than a few major surgeries. Prior to her kidney cancer diagnosis in the early 1990's, she was relatively healthy, other than her escalation of cigarette-induced emphysema. But with the surgical removal of her tumor, subsequent cancer recurrence, and abdominal adhesions, necessary hospitalizations became more frequent. She hated being there, and voiced strong but pleasant desires for discharge, even on those days immediately following major surgery. She felt recuperation was much better served while resting in one's own bed and being served chicken noodle soup from a ladle held by loving hands. Oftentimes, my mom's longing to go home did not coincide with the physician's plan, but that didn't stop her from making her wishes known. Once my mom decided it was time for her to be discharged, physicians had a hard time disagreeing.

On those days, long before the early morning doctor rounds, my mom would simply remove her hospital gown and put on her own clothes: pantyhose, loafers and all. As the physician team entered her room to assess her, pulling back her covers for examination sent a strong and clear message. Yes, she was going home. Combined with her smile, her accessible charm, and that finger pointing accompanied by her eye twinkle, her resolution was hard to counter. Indeed, coming home meant she healed quicker and was just plain happier.

During his last physical therapy session at the RIC, Kathy and Phil sent a video of Conor flanked by the support of Phil and Joe, the physical therapist, on the track just outside the RIC. He walked with support over 150 feet, and THAT felt like a miracle. Conventional wisdom would say that the process of learning to walk again was the product of months of tedious and creative measures by the physical therapy team at the RIC. Indeed, their methods of strengthening and conditioning Conor's mind and muscles were instrumental in the process of Conor learning how to walk again. And the final RIC memory of him walking, even with significant assistance, left a promising hope that Conor would eventually regain his ability to walk independently. We were hopeful the process of additional therapy would yield more stamina over time. Progress in the world of TBI is generally at a snail's pace, but we were about to be blown away. Just two days after his return home, Kathy sent a video of Conor climbing the stairs.

Without the video and ability to see firsthand, I would not have believed it. Conor, without assistance, climbed the steps two at a time. Yes, two at a time. Jack and Phil could hardly keep up with him. The scene was akin to Lazarus rising from the dead: unbelievable and miraculous all at the same time. We could hardly contain our joy. This was a direct sign from Conor that although words still eluded him, he was ready to get started on the road to recovery. As he owned the familiar staircase once again, the proof was evident. Home offered the best environment for healing. My mom was right after all.

Kathy became a full-time tutor upon Conor's return. She couldn't rest in helplessness or fear, as there was healing to be done. And she felt she couldn't be wasting time. She described herself as a bit manic, becoming rigid in Conor's need for a schedule, and her need to make everything— I mean *everything*—purposeful.

July 2, 2013 PRFC

Imagine this scene. Kathy and Conor are in the kitchen. Conor is sitting in his wheelchair (which he has not done much of today since he seems to prefer walking). Kathy says to Conor "Listen mister, since you are here for dinner every night you need to help with the dishes." So, Conor stands from his wheelchair, takes a cup that Kathy hands to him and proceeds to place it in the top level of the dishwasher. Then came the dishes, one at a time placed appropriately on the lower rack. That scene to me says so many things. First of all, Kathy and Conor are establishing a new life together based on their incredible mutual love. My sister (always the educator) sees every life situation as a learning tool. Conor has his work cut out for him, and I anticipate even the smallest of daily living tasks will provide therapeutic value in the Crippen household. Second, there is delight in the mundane. Who would have thought that loading a dishwasher would be such a triumphant experience? And finally, despite the occurrence of a traumatic brain injury, chores are not easily dismissed in the Crippen house.... There is a sure confidence we have gained these last 3½ months in the presence of God and the air of hope that the Spirit provides. Sometimes, if you take a moment to take stock, you realize that the mud isn't quite as deep and the trail is lined with more tangible hope. We don't have our heads in the sand, but it just feels

good to call progress what it is…and we are sticking with
just that. With hope and prayer for tomorrow, and gratitude
for it all… Go Conor Go.

The bravado of my words planted engaging optimism, and met the expectation from all participants, near and far, that Conor's story continued to embody inspiration and hope. The reality was, we did have our heads in the sand. Healing from TBI can be a mammoth undertaking that takes years, but all Kathy could do was take one day at a time and rest in the smallest of victories like loading cups in a dishwasher. Looking beyond the challenge of each day was too overwhelming, and Kathy was still too apprehensive. So, instead, Kathy's gladness came from looking back. Within a week, Conor no longer needed a wheelchair in the house, and he was able to help with the dishes. That was progress. The charge was to rest in the present, delight in the simple successes, and believe that one improvement would lead to another.

Still, being home felt surreal for Kathy. Who can ever imagine such a profound alteration in the trajectory of life? Her ordinary routines, freedom to craft her own schedules, and the absence of immense responsibility were now in a former life. Now, every waking minute was for the intention of Conor's recovery. The days of lamenting the small stuff were gone. The demands for creativity in "lesson planning" yielded new heartache for her, yet there was a transcending theme to the story of Conor's brain injury. All of us—but especially the Crippens—were part of a narrative that was sacred, fed by a spiritual energy we may assuredly have missed, had we not been propelled into this uninvited story. Whether the angels of our hearts were carrying the Crippens, or Conor was truly meant to overcome this indescribable adversity, we felt we were within a movement that was pretty remarkable. *What more could we want?* I wrote on July 7. Later that night, we would be reminded of the fragility of Conor's state.

⇜ chapter 19 ⇝

It was Bridget's turn to sleep on the couch next to Conor. As she settled in for the night around 9:00 p.m., Conor began to seize. Witnessing a seizure is awful, especially when unexpected. The images of eyes rolling back into the head, and the rapid, violent jerks that overrun the body is nothing short of traumatic. This night, Conor seized not once, but twice, shattering the delicate momentum of his progress since coming home. His unexpected seizing caused alarm and immediately put the family back into a state of crisis.

My cell phone rang. I answered, knowing it was Kathy. I heard the panic and fear in her voice. My heart plummeted in that now-familiar feeling of dread.

"Conor had a seizure," she said. Her breathlessness and high-pitched alarm transferred to the lump growing in my throat. "He's on his way to the ER by ambulance," she continued.

I prayed with fierce desperation as Mark and I drove to meet them. I pushed sentiments of anger deep beneath my charge to provide support to my sister. Again, I wondered where fairness reigned in her life blueprint, yet I also realized that resignation to victimhood did no one any good, especially Conor, who was fighting his way back to life. As I made my way to her side, I organized my epicenter so that I could offer comfort based in unbending belief that, although this was a setback, no seizure could derail Conor—or any Crippen, for that matter.

I entered the hospital emergency room to see Kathy distraught and filled with fear. Despite the fact that seizures are a common occurrence in the aftermath of TBI, Conor hadn't exhibited seizure activity to this point, so the onset of this condition felt random and startling. Mark offered reassurance, based on his ability to navigate the emergency department medical scene, and enveloped my sister in his arms. I stood with Bridget, still shaking from the ordeal.

The return to the emergency room was startling and unsettling. The sound of monitors and the high-pitched beeps threatened to suck the fresh air of progress since Conor's return home. His arms, finally healed from daily needle-sticks, were punctured again with a catheter attached to IV fluid. My sister's hands encased those of her son, whose inability to fully comprehend this return to the clinical setting was palpable. He was restless, despite the anti-seizure medications now flowing through his veins. Bridget's tears purged her fear. Phil stood on the other side of Conor, giving words of encouragement and comfort. All hope since coming home felt lost, hijacked by the ferocious reminder that recovery from this TBI would never be easy. The road would never be smooth or predictable. This loving and determined family would be at the mercy of the unexpected and unwelcome yet again. I stood, feeling nauseated at the witness of angst I saw worn by my sister and her family. Their legs of strength were shaky. Once again, I felt helpless as I stood in the shadow of my sister. I wondered how much more she could take.

My default action was to engage our community of supporters again in a plea for prayer. I knew hundreds of our followers would show up via social media, offering positive and prayerful energy for Conor and his family. The outreach of those who could believe when Kathy and Phil doubted was needed. Often, my intention in writing on Conor's page was to help most my sister, who was in the midst of another long night.

July 9, 2013 PRFC

Yesterday was perhaps the most trying day for the Crippens. As I spoke to my sister, she said that yesterday was even more difficult than March 16, when Conor experienced his accident. Yesterday was not obviously blanketed in anything good. We have spoken often of the transcending energy that has been present since day one, allowing the Crippens to remain lifted by the evident grace of God. Looking back, such tangible flow of love moved Kathy and Phil one day to the next, supported by faith and hope. There were days when the flow was desperate, but God evidently showed up. As I mentioned weeks ago, there has not been a day where hope did not meet us at sunset.

I guess tough days need to simply be noted. And some days cannot be reconciled by easy answers or evident lack of God's presence. Let's just leave yesterday and name it honestly. It was unexpected, painful, frustrating, and long. It is good to name such days, but that is not where we rest. Today, Conor is back on track. Of course, he is now on anti-seizure medication, but his home routine has not missed a beat (other than Phil and Kathy still on pins and needles a bit). Kathy and Phil logistically worked the day, gaining information from those docs in Chicago and facilitating new opportunities for information in Columbus and Dayton. There is no time to let weeds grow under their feet as they are in the business of Conor's healing.

The fact that Conor had a very restful night and his day has been quite ordinary has not gone spiritually unnoticed by my sister. As we talked, I said to her that God indeed answered prayers as Conor had a restful night and did not have any apparent damage from his seizures (he still walked the kitchen with his mom today). And so it was. I said to Kathy that God has carried Conor thus far and He will not abandon him. Kathy's response was that she wasn't quite so sure as they resisted fear and anxiety in the emergency room in the middle of yet another dark night. There is room for anger, doubt, and heartbreaking fatigue. A new day always comes, however, bringing a new opportunity to begin again. Although the Crippens are cautious, they once again choose hope and light and healing. They simply picked up where they left off, despite their worry and fatigue. Once again, they chose to put all unproductive energy aside as their love for Conor and trust in this process trump all. So, we are back in the realm of miraculous possibility. Conor makes it possible to easily return to that realm. His essence shines brighter than any despair. As I said, there has not been a day where hope has not met us at sunset, and that remains true. With exciting hope for tomorrow and gratitude for all of you who lifted us yesterday... Go Conor Go!!!

Hope did indeed meet us at sunrise following Conor's seizure incident. Our cyber community met the Crippens in their despair with words of encouragement and love. The blanket of support wrapped them with snug intention, and the light of the day gave clarity. Clinically speaking, seizures result from a sudden surge of electrical activity in the brain. Medical reports that Conor's seizures didn't further damage the brain did little to calm the waters of worry; however, divine providence had the last word, literally.

Two days after Conor's seizure, he started talking. Kathy heard Conor say, "Mom," followed by, "I love mom." Just like when he conquered his staircase, Conor's ability to talk…simply surfaced. Upon command, he repeated words. They pointed to objects in the house, named them, and then heard the sweet sound of Conor's hoarse voice repeating the name of everything in their midst. "Table…pencil…sink…fork…" Hearing him whisper "love you too," or "hi Dad," or "Bridget" brought new meaning to the power of words. We went from one WOW moment to another as we experienced and heard Conor regaining his voice. Perhaps his seizures released some of the traumatic energy, making room for discovery and restoration. Who knows? We really didn't need a medical expert to support what we knew for sure was another miracle.

It didn't take long to get back on the hope wagon. The Crippen village of supporters were instrumental in reminding us that love permeated every fiber of this story. I was at my sister's house two days following Conor's seizures. Just before dinnertime, the doorbell rang. There was a familiar friend offering a basket of support. It was a meal, prepared so that Kathy need only reheat and serve. I remember the beautiful aura surrounding the basket; the smell of comfort and a reflection of the warmth and positive energy of the meal-maker. Her hug for Kathy exuded the kind of provision that propels us forward.

There were many who brought sustenance for the Crippens. Outreach for those navigating rough roads in life can feel futile when you want nothing more than to help make things better. Short of healing the sick or eliminating pain, preparing a meal is such a tender way of saying "I care."

Day after day, as dinners were brought to my sister's family, I witnessed the affection that accompanied the foil-covered Pyrex dishes. A meal to a friend in need brings a token of a greater concentric circle of love, which seeps into that which is broken. Tangible love is expressed through casseroles and trays of chocolate chip cookies. The smiles and hugs of those who prepare them remind us that the world still turns, the sun still shines, and that the burden of life's hard yoke can be made lighter, by the fact that someone cared enough to cook for you. This accident gave us new eyes to see these people we had known, or barely knew, who showed up in prayer or purpose. It was humbling to be the recipient of such outpouring as my sister remained in this perpetual state of embrace.

Community fundraisers, prepared meals, or prayers for Conor's healing felt like the stilts giving lift to the Crippen journey, and helped to propel them forward. Even in the shadow of Conor's seizure episode, he was making small strides. He started eating vitamin- and nutrient-packed smoothies instead of relying on feeding through his G-tube. His stamina for walking improved, and his words returned. We were called to appreciate his restoration of life. Each day offered the blessing of improvement by comparing it to the day before. Simple pleasures, like sleeping in his own bed, were mind-boggling.

July 22, 2013 PRFC

In anticipation of Conor's homecoming just over three weeks ago, several pieces of medical equipment were delivered to the Crippen house to facilitate an easier life at home. First there was a wheelchair, which is now history as of last week. Conor has so quickly regained his leg strength and balance, and now he walks purposefully not only around his house. Also, there was a hospital bed delivered and set up in the Crippen den, which has been Conor's temporary place of resting and sleeping since he came home. We thought navigating stairs would be a challenge, and then all of a sudden, he was walking up and down the stairs unaided. Last night, Conor slept upstairs in his own bed. As my sister looked at the hospital bed in their den this morning, she made the bold but confident decision that the den was no longer Conor's place of rest. From here on out, he would sleep where he was meant to sleep—in his own bed, in his own room—and that hospital bed would soon be making its way back to medical equipment land. So just like that, Conor moves on.

Such progress is good for the family soul. There is an intangible joy for Kathy and Phil, knowing their kids are where they are meant to be. I think any of us who are parents to college-aged kids have a sense of peace when they are home and sleep in their own beds. As these kids navigate their way in an emerging world, coming home and being revitalized by family love and energy makes any mom or dad feel good. We can certainly say that Conor's journey to his own room and the ability to sleep in his own bed has been remarkable. I can remember, way back in the spring, my sister and I having a conversation during which her longing for Conor to come home for the summer (like all his peers were preparing to do) was palpable. As I saw the ruffled sheets and randomly placed pillows on Conor's bed this morning after his good night's sleep, I met my sister in her joy. I can only imagine what is merely a dream for Conor today will be reality in no time. That is just how Conor does things. So, we continue to pray for his ability to remain attentive and less restless. It will surely come. Go Conor Go!

. . . . .

In the weeks following Conor's homecoming, he was restless. He paced constantly stemming from his brain's inability to process movement in an orderly way. As a result, he was up and down, up and down. We would learn later that his early fidgetiness and aimless walking were due to the brain's electrical volatility and lack of brain inhibition. Damaged brains are excitable. Due to his lingering unsteadiness, we all took turns walking with him as he wandered the house, offering a hand to help him with balance. The look in his eye was still blank. Therapy sessions with Ohio State University were not yet in full swing, but my sister—in her need for more—was already pursuing other options for treatment. She felt each day without purpose was a wasted opportunity for Conor. Her mind was racing with problem solving possibilities. She accessed her mental Rolodex for anyone she might call for help in establishing new momentum for Conor's healing. Specifically, Kathy tried to think of those she knew through her professional experience as a teacher, and that is when Ann Anzalone came to mind. *Why not?* This was Kathy's constant mantra, which threw fear to the wind. Calling Ann offered nothing to lose.

A dynamic motivational speaker and educator, Ann facilitated several workshops for educators in Kathy's school district. Once a teacher to special needs children, Ann counseled educators and parents in finding new ways to reach those who were struggling to learn. In the early 1980's Ann came upon a book, *Unicorns are Real* by Barbara Meister Vitale, which offered simple explanations regarding the different functions of the brain's hemispheres. Characteristics of right- and left-brain workings helped educators like Ann design educational tools to reach those with different learning preferences. She became an expert in right-brain learning, often helping those who had trouble expanding their capacity to absorb information. From there she discovered the connection between movement and brain communication. For example, moving an arm in a figure-eight pattern is like sending a text message in the brain. Her practical application for addressing all learning styles helped to make her a well-sought speaker in the Dayton area. Ann answered Kathy's call, agreed to help, and was the first person to offer my sister an expanded understanding of brain rehabilitation.

Ann Anzalone gives new meaning to the word lively. Slight in stature, her infectious energy can be likened to that of a new puppy. Her initial assessment of Conor was quick and clear. She touched his forehead, arms, and legs with quick taps. She said Conor's mind, body, and soul were all disconnected due to his severe trauma. She looked at Conor's vacant look and said, "We need to bring him home."

Her demeanor was matter-of-fact in hope. Her energy, spitfire character, and ability to take control of Conor's environment set a new tone that would provide the basis for the rest of the healing journey. Finally, for Kathy, understanding that the brain needed to heal from the inside out made sense.

Those early sessions with Ann provided the beginning of education into neuroplasticity and kinesiology. The basic premise is this: movement using opposition, meaning opposite sides of the body working together, has proven to be an effective way to re-integrate the mind and the body. When a baby learns to crawl, communication between the left and right sides of the brain occur, facilitating electrical impulses to pass freely between the two. This is a learned process as an infant, and is the basis of subsequent abilities to walk and run. Following trauma, the brain is capable of rehabilitation, first, by reestablishing the capability to perform opposing motion. This simple act of contralateral movement—i.e., left arm with right leg or right leg with left arm—helps to re-program the neurological system.[4] Crawling makes balance possible. Once balance is restored, brain cells and nerves can establish more complex capabilities.

Conor's brain's ability to communicate had become confused, resulting in neurological disorganization and an inability for information to flow in an ordinary way. The shearing of his brain connections had been so severe, there was no ability for his nerve fibers to cooperate with one another, affecting virtually every ability to function at a higher level.

Ann recognized that Conor needed to begin his healing from the base up. In other words, his brain needed the act of crawling again to initiate healing. So, where did she begin? By passively moving his arms and legs in a contralateral way. Mimicking the act of crawling, or in figure-eight configurations, facilitated new communication between the right and left parts of the brain. Finally, something made sense to Kathy, who had spent her entire professional career trying to navigate pathways of the mind to better understand her students. Ann spoke the language my sister could understand. The opportunity to incorporate years of learning now for the benefit of her own son suddenly gave new charge to tutoring.

The mind is a complex entity. Configuring a therapy regime that could bring back Conor's ability to function required the recognition that his injury was not just physical, but affected his emotional and mental state as well. Ann's suggestion of a more holistic approach to healing opened the realm of thought regarding therapeutic interventions. Hence, creativity exploded

---

[4] "Chapter 15." *Brain Lash Maximize Your Recovery from Mild Brain Injury,* by PhD Gail L. Denton, Demos Health, 2008, pp. 124–128.

from the non-conventional mind of my sister. Now, the schedule of these initial days was filled with renewed purpose. Ann's plan also broadened Kathy's scope of understanding. Suddenly, the Crippen kitchen was filled with white boards, markers, schedules, workbooks, music, and "assignments" for Conor to do throughout the day. Her lesson plans were laced with laughter, hugs, encouragement, and the ultimate belief that they were in the realm of real possibilities. Although they would pursue traditional physical, occupational, and speech therapies at The Ohio State University, the expanded mission of healing Conor's brain from the inside out and from the bottom up provided the path that made most sense.

Ann also challenged Kathy on the component of nutrition. Throughout Conor's recovery in Chicago, Conor received G-tube feedings four times a day, which consisted of 8 oz. of a vanilla-colored *who knows what it is* liquid. This was the mainstream nutrition-supplement brand served to hospital patients. Components of this "complete and balanced" nutrition included corn maltodextrin, corn oil, gum arabic and fructooligosaccharides—whatever that means. Most ingredients weren't recognizable, which led Kathy to begin her investigation for healthier nutritional supplementation with more familiar natural components.

Dayton, Ohio might not offer the tourist attractions of cities like New York or San Francisco, but as a lifelong resident of Dayton, I could argue we have the best place to raise a family, impressive biking trails, and sunsets that rival the French Riviera. There is no argument, however, that Dayton is home to the nation's unsurpassed locally owned grocery store, Dorothy Lane Market (locally—and lovingly—referred to as "DLM"). Attention to customer service, family-centered philosophy, and highest-quality options for food make this store one of Dayton,

Ohio's best business establishments. To regular patrons, DLM employees become like family. Also, luckily for Kathy, patrons of DLM benefit from a truly extraordinary selection of groceries.

Shortly after Ann challenged Kathy to take a better look at Conor's nutritional intake, Kathy was shopping at DLM. After talking with an employee in the Healthy Living department, Kathy became aware of an alternative brand of tube-feeding supplement. Liquid Hope, an oral meal replacement, is a liquid nutritional meal packed with organic ingredients such as garbanzo beans, brown rice, vitamins, and kale. Robin Gentry McGee, a fellow Daytonian, formulated Liquid Hope to provide quality nutrition for her father after he suffered a brain injury, and thereafter formed a company, Functional Formularies, to market the nutritional meal replacement. Compared with the unpronounceable ingredients the hospital brand liquid meals, for Kathy, buying a case of Liquid Hope was a no-brainer.

My sister was finding her way in how to best help Conor. Crafting a mosaic of healing options began with the understanding that the brain could heal itself. Moving Conor's arms in figure-eight configurations and providing nutrition that made sense empowered her to seek more. She was part of a blind trust, not really knowing what the next step would be. There were no blueprints of design for recovery from brain injury, so she just did what Kathy has always done. She kept her mind open, her heart grounded in gratitude, and arms outstretched to the goodness this journey yielded. All she knew for sure was the mission to seek and remain open to all possibilities that could help Conor. And she was just getting started. Within weeks, Conor was doing yoga, massage therapy, and acupuncture, each with therapists who quickly bought into the magic of this Crippen story. The desire to be part of this healing journey was infectious.

One of the reasons Conor's journey was so remarkable was that on any given day, God's graces felt like raindrops falling from the sky. Whereas gratitude could rest in the touch of one such raindrop, the act of awareness means an entire pool of goodness is suddenly resting in the palm of your hand. And all you had to do was just remain still enough to watch.

On one of these such days, Fr. Patrick visited, on his way to a conference at Xavier University. Dayton falls along the route, so he spent the afternoon with the Crippens, and we joined them for a celebration of Mass in their family room. I sat slightly behind Conor, who was seated next to Fr. Patrick. I looked at Conor. His recent hair growth almost concealed the scars that reminded us of how far he'd come. The severity of this catastrophic injury, the meticulous care of his Chicago medical team, and the conscious decision to hope every day now brought him to this place. As I listened to the Gospel read by Fr. Patrick about God's ability to answer prayer, I realized that although we weren't there quite yet, I trusted that someday Conor's scars would be like any other scar; a reminder of a hurt that has been long overcome. Conor participated in the sacredness of the liturgy by making the Sign of the Cross, saying Amen, sharing in the sign of peace, and receiving Communion for the first time in months. I was overcome with how far the Crippen family had come. I connected the hopefulness of this day with those of the past months, filled with unknown and fear. Although this presented the greatest life challenge for them, the Crippen commitment to not bow to fear or succumb to doubt remained steadfast.

That day, too, offered the rebirth of Conor's smile. Prior to his accident, his smile presented with such grand expression and joy, yet his face had remained expressionless ever since. But then we noticed the corner of his mouth turned upward and his eyes reflected a hint of a twinkle. Yes, he was still in there. The rain kept pouring grace. Some days, I couldn't keep up with the gratitude for each drop, but the overflowing waters of God's touch on this day left us all filled with wonder. Fr. Patrick was a reminder that trust in healing far exceeded the confines of the Crippen home. This day offered an opportunity to rest, but not for too long. Conor's story of recovery continued to unfold with purpose and intention.

☙ chapter 20 ☙

By mid-summer, daily schedules defined all hours of the day, including sleep time. The trauma of Conor' seizure episode waned as he adjusted to his anti-seizure medication. I was in constant contact with my sister, delighting in her updates of Conor's mind reclamation. One misconception of brain injury is that because of such trauma, the person becomes simple-minded. This is the furthest from truth. The content of an injured person's mind remains, but the challenge is clearing away the debris of injury so that new pathways can access the full essence of the person. It was hard to reason why Conor couldn't articulate quite yet in conversation, but he could correctly identify chemical symbols on the Periodic Table. He could sing along to lyrics of his favorite songs, but he couldn't remember his recent experiences at Loyola. Conor was always a deep thinker, one who embraced challenge of thought, and who instinctively articulated the language of the profound. He was quick to access certain compartments of knowledge he'd once mastered in his science-oriented mind. He was also pretty comical. So, as his voice returned, Kathy probed him with the sorts of questions he thrived on. This was a text I received on July 30, 2013:

Asking Conor 20 questions:
Kathy: love is….
Conor: equal to hope

Kathy: our family is special because....
Conor: I'm in it

To which Kathy followed up, "No worry about self-esteem here!"

Jack reported also this day, "Conor just looked in the mirror and said, 'Damn, I look good.'" Truly, no self-esteem issues.

Conor's high school friends showed up at the Crippen house daily. They were unafraid to step onto the coals of the uncomfortable regarding their friend's brain injury. They gathered in the Crippen basement, laughing and reminiscing about high school years. They were themselves and spoke to him as if nothing had changed. Conor listened, giving a thumb's up. This presence of old friends, mixed with Crippen family love and Conor's determination, all supported by the tangible evidence of grace, propelled us within this new flow of hope. This was the new ordinary time. We overheard laughter coming from his bedroom, and saw his flat affect brighten when friends were in the house. The fruition of Conor's loyalties and kindnesses coming back to him in his time of need lifted my sister each day. There was a whole drove of kids who didn't even knock upon entering the Crippen home. They were welcome any time to come and bring their unique brand of healing. Underlying every moment was the profound awareness that Conor's mere survival defied every odd. "Friend therapy" was just as important for Conor as any other organized session. Their belief that Conor could overcome was solid. I was humbled by the commitment to friendship and the loyal companionship these 18- and 19-year-olds consistently displayed. As Conor hung out with his friends, the light in his eyes continued to brighten within the air of mutual friendship. Their simple time together bred life-giving energy not only for

Conor, but for his friends as well. They gave loving nourishment and encouragement, and in return he gave back a lesson in triumph and an example of what it means to overcome. Kathy and I talked of this mutual blessing which would feed them for a lifetime.

As August welcomed the symphony of cricket song, the ending of summer felt just around the bend. Soon, Conor's friends would be returning to college. Kathy often said she felt like she was sending the Alter High School Class of 2012 off to college as so many from Conor's class prioritized their summer with visits to the Crippen home. Their normal time with Conor, walking beside him as he roamed with restlessness and encouraging him to drink his nutritional smoothies, offered an ordinary flavor to this profoundly unordinary journey of healing. They provided a bridge, connecting the essence of Conor with the potential to get better. When Conor came home, the fearlessness and integrity of these kids—unafraid to look their distant friend in the eye—provided Kathy and Phil with hope of the best kind: youth. Their persistence and willingness to show up gave blessing to Conor's recovery process. They showed up again and again with smiles, knowledge, and love for him. Their testimony of how Conor's essence touched them allowed, in turn, reciprocal healing for Conor. It was a win-win. But then the new school year called them to resume their own lives of personal and academic growth.

August 9, 2013 PRFC

Although my sister and I talk daily, sometimes it is a good thing when we can really catch up. And I have to admit, usually those catch-up talks are over a glass of wine. Late yesterday afternoon when Conor's great friends were just hanging at the Crippen house, Kathy and I were able to sit outside on her porch and relax for a few minutes. As the Crippens are fully vested in Conor's healing journey, Kathy and Phil share the foundational energy that supports the rest of us who are able to remain so upbeat and hopeful on this long and winding road. Every once in a while, however, I just need to look my sister in the eye and make sure she truly is doing OK. We have walked a few other mountain treks together in this life of sisterhood, and I know Kathy pretty well. One of her most beautiful attributes is that she is not afraid to share her heart. My brother Gerry knows that when our sister feels passion, joy, sorrow, happiness or hurt, she lets it all flow, which makes her so accessible to others. Since March 16, however, Kathy has remained in the light of Conor's healing. It is not often she allows herself to slip into anything that would detract her energy away from love and hope for her son. When she does have those moments of sadness, they come from a place of just missing Conor. His great friends come and go; they are preparing to return to college, and although Conor will get there one day, I think the longing of Conor pre-accident seeps from her heart. So yesterday, she allowed herself just a moment of sadness. While sharing the morning hours with Conor, this mother's love got the best of her. As she sat with Conor and told him how much she loved him and that she was just missing him, Conor did what he has always done. Despite the injury and continued healing of his brain, that essence and willingness to transcend to a place of intuitive love for his mom was revealed. In his ability to articulate the healing love she so needed in that moment, her faith and resolve was restored to full throttle. The energy between them has always reflected this love and intent to understand life's purpose and meaning. There is a language they share that is still communicated freely between them, and which enables Kathy to remain in the light. As I looked at my sister's face yesterday, still so soft and porous in this challenge, I loved her even more.

As we sat together outside, Kathy again talked of God's grace, which has profoundly carried her these last 5 months. I, too, know that God's hand has cradled her so that she can continue to flow nothing but goodness. I can't help but think of our mom. There was no greater teacher of how to love. I see her spirit flow through Kathy each and every day. Perhaps it is our mom that is reflected in the light of my sister's eyes. Our heavenly family remains alive and well in support of Conor and our family. As the rain gently began to fall yesterday while sitting outside together, my sister and I looked at one another and smiled. We were in no hurry to rush inside; rather, we chose to remain within the space of the falling raindrops. It is sort of metaphorical, now that I think about it. The space between us, between the heavens, and between the gentle drops reflected a sacredness which remains with me today. A little bit of rain soaking felt good. We continue to pray boldly. Go Conor Go.

⚜ chapter 21 ⚜

Three times a week, Conor was scheduled for therapy sessions at The Ohio State University Dodd Rehabilitation Center in Columbus. I offered to take Conor on Wednesdays, which then became our "date" afternoons, giving my sister an opportunity for some solitude. Driving the hour-and-fifteen-minute trip offered companionship time. Being with Conor was always uplifting, but being with him as his brain fibers reconnected left me amazed. I noticed each week slight improvements as we talked about music, the exits off of I-70, the cities east and west of Dayton. We talked about the universe, the stars, and the planets. As I drove, the opportunity to share ordinary conversation with Conor blew me away every time. Simple moments offered abundant opportunity for gratitude. Wednesday afternoons also gave Ben and Holly, students at OSU, a chance to observe and encourage Conor.

August 28, 2013 PRFC

I love Wednesdays. It has become my day to bring Conor to therapy, as it gives my sister an afternoon to touch base with her school and to be in the teaching environment that she loves so much. It also gives me a chance to be with Conor, see his therapy progress, and just enjoy being with him. Today, we drove to Columbus singing Jimmy Buffett's version of "Brown Eyed Girl." That could have easily been the highlight of my day, until I witnessed Conor in therapy.

I have to say, first of all, Conor works hard. Although that is not surprising to any of us who know him, seeing him try again and again to perform the tasks asked of him is awe-inspiring. There have been many therapy sessions in the past when the therapists would ask Conor to do something, and you could tell he had a hard time either concentrating, remembering what it was they asked of him, or simply remembering how to do such a simple thing. Today, however, Conor was on task and nailed it all. Multitasking in an obstacle course designed to challenge his ability to "multi-function" with physical and cognitive therapies was very doable for him today. Sorting a deck of cards into four different suit piles was done in 9 minutes, much quicker than last time (with his left hand, no less). Yet these tasks are not without effort, as evidenced by his sweat and need to rest his head in his hands from time to time.

Such is the world of therapy; small steps of hard work through various physical, occupational, and speech therapies. The exceptional outpatient unit at OSU is filled with those who are trying to negotiate a life event that leaves them compromised in one way or another. Some deficits are very obvious, some are not. There was a man today learning how to use two new prosthetics, as both legs were amputated above the knee. There were people there young and old, all being attended to by dedicated and creative therapists who are trained and willing to believe in the power of recovery through hard work and dedication. Their encouragement, professional training, and challenge in unlocking each unique patient bodes deep respect. And although I am probably a bit biased, I think Conor's therapists love working with him and see an endless horizon of hope for him.

I was so happy to have Ben and Holly meet me at Conor's therapy sessions. It is more fun when there are other eyes reflecting the awe so evident. It is that nod of the head, followed by the sure smile, when observing Conor shatter his own therapy ceiling that is just more fun to share. Ben, Holly, and I had quite a few communal looks of knowing and celebration.

We have the blessing of time. Conor continues to improve every day. It is slow, it feels sometimes like a turtle's pace, but it is certain and true. As I wrap up my words with you tonight, I pray that those patients who underwent therapy at OSU today have the same feeling of hope as we do with Conor. And to all you therapists out there, we value and admire your calling. Go Conor Go.

Kathy and I often said that somehow, in the course of Conor's comatose state while in the SICU, my mom took residence in his spirit. If you had the pleasure of knowing her, you'd remember clearly the strength of her hands. Her signature reach for whoever was next to her offered connection in a quick but firm squeeze. Often, there were no words to accompany her loving touch, as the strength of her grasp spoke of her unyielding love. So many times, as I sat by her side she would offer her hand, palm up, so that without even a thought, I would slip my hand into hers. Her grip met me wherever my heart met my soul. I still feel that love that was so readily available in her touch. Now that Conor and I spent so much time in the car chatting about the insignificant, he, too, would reach his hand over to me, palm up, just like my mom used to do. All those years my mom held Conor's hand while walking him to the bus stop must have sealed him with her brand. Every time I slipped my hand into his I felt my mom in between us both. And every time, I smiled, sending a note of silent thanks to the heavens.

As is the case with recovery, simple advances speak volumes. That exceptional part of Conor was resurfacing. I saw it when he was with his mom, reassuring her he would be okay. I saw it with his friends as he reminded them of the power of reciprocal loyalty. I saw his ability to connect with others as he greeted the doormen and receptionists at OSU with smiles and salutations of joy. His intention in reaching out always made him unique, yet to see and feel such connection restored in his recovery made our hearts sing with joy. Some doctors along the way said Conor's brain injury possibly threatened his ability to feel and express emotion. But when I met his outstretched hand as he asked me if I was okay, I felt the promise of even greater healing as his spirit unfolded like a blooming flower, one petal at a time.

Crafting Conor's healing journey required Kathy and Phil to remain dedicated to the here and now. Yet the memories of him unable to hold his head up proved how far he'd come. The tumultuous sequence of events over the past five months was extraordinary. One day Conor was like any other freshman in college, and the next, his ability to function with any level of consciousness was wiped away. Now, with each passing day, defiance of expectation gained speed. The strides felt enormous, but when compared to how Conor lived life pre-accident, the work to be done felt arduous. Yes, Conor was walking; although aimless and restless. Yes, he was talking. Yes, he could follow simple commands; and yes, Conor's improvements thus far had defied all clinical odds. But the goals were far from achieved. The work needed to unlock higher-level brain function was considerable. As Conor and his therapists at OSU cultivated professional relationships grounded in promise, I thought of Fr. Patrick and his timeless advice to maintain an attitude of faith in Conor's caregivers. Conor's charm and essence, yet again, transcended the fragmented fibers of his brain. Traditional therapy was instrumental, but my sister, ever hungry for more, began to think outside the customary paradigm of brain rehabilitation. This would become her signature, and would take Conor to places unimagined.

· · · · ·

In the months following Conor's accident, among his deficits was a right-arm tremor, impeding and cumbersome as he worked to strengthen peripheral limb function. Right-hand dominant, his abilities to eat, write, carry, or perform even mundane small motor tasks were hindered by the constant shakiness of his hand. Feeling that the tremor was a hindrance in Conor's ability to progress in rehabilitation, Kathy sought some medical advice. Recommended to her was a neurologist at the Rush Medical Center in Chicago; this physician was well known for his work with Parkinson's Disease and associated tremors. Mark and I offered to take Conor to his Chicago appointment, for not only would our excursion back to Chicago give Kathy and Phil a break, Mark could also ask better questions of the neurologist. And so, we set off on the familiar drive up I-65 through Indiana, with Conor engaging in conversation ranging from the solar system to the next opportunity for lake-time.

Following an assessment and a plethora of questions for Conor, the neurologist's professional recommendation was that Conor work on compensating right-hand limitations with left-hand training. In other words, deal with it. Other than a longshot attempt at deep brain stimulation the M.D. had nothing else to offer.[5]

[5] Lyons, Kelly E., and Rajesh Pahwa. "Deep Brain Stimulation and Essential Tremor." *Journal of Clinical Neurophysiology*, vol. 21, no. 1, 2004, pp. 2–5., doi:10.1097/00004691-200401000-00002.

The lack of treatment recommendations felt like a dead end, one not easily accepted by my sister. Mainstream approaches to TBI rehabilitation felt incomplete and sometimes short-sighted. Over and over again, the message was to get used to it, learn to live with it, and other suggestions of resignation. Still vibrating were the words, *You can never leave him alone...he won't know what to do if the house is on fire.* But my sister didn't spend much time lamenting. Nor was she discouraged by the suggestion to "just accept it." There was no room for acceptance when trust led the way.

Dr. David Heuser joined Conor's team in the fall of 2013, following a serendipitous recommendation. During a Saturday afternoon wine tasting at DLM, Mark and I ran into the husband of Mark's former patient who had died several years prior. Remarried now, this retired physics professor from the University of Dayton introduced us to his new wife, Lucy. We chatted about incidental things while sipping, and then Mark and I brought up Conor, the eventual pivot to all conversation these days. We just never knew how random connection could yield an expansion of possibility for him. In this case, it did—in a big way. Lucy, who worked for a local chiropractor, referred us to Dr. David Heuser, a Chiropractic Functional Neurologist whose office was just down the road in Kettering, Ohio. I knew Kathy was open to investigating all possibilities for treatment, so I took notes and forwarded them to her.

The timing of Dr. Heuser's introduction couldn't have been better. Kathy's desire to expand Conor's therapeutic interventions was growing. The customary approach to TBI rehab being done at OSU was fine, but Kathy knew there had to be other methods out there to encourage the holistic approach to healing that Ann Anzalone purported. The occupational therapeutic goals of how quickly Conor could assemble a puzzle or find items in a grocery store was fine, but Kathy felt something more could be done. As an educator, her career was based on creativity in expanding the mind capabilities of children with varied learning disabilities. Certainly, the charge to meet Conor's needs could not be limited by conventional thought alone. She felt more could be done. She called his office the next day.

Kathy and Conor drove to Dr. Heuser's office located in a dated strip mall that was marked by a simple sign above the front door: **CHIROPRACTOR**. Kathy parked the car just in front of the entrance and looked at Conor. Both had raised eyebrows; Kathy said, "Let's just check it out, Conor, just this once."

Upon entering the waiting room, Kathy recalls being disarmed by the unassuming aura of the modest office surroundings. There was no formality or division of hierarchy, as is often felt in the air of professional medical settings. Rather, patients were met with an openness and fluidity of purpose in the open therapy room, and the welcome was reinforced by the smiles and positive demeanor of the staff. Dr. Heuser, or "Doc," as we came to affectionately call him, and his wife, Dr. Denise Logan (both trained in Chiropractic Neurology) moved about the room with unpretentious clinical intention, tending and then re-tending to their patients as their staff worked with each person: moving, stretching, and stimulating the body's natural ability to heal itself.

At first impression, Doc was down-to-earth and accessible. His huge smile and sense of humor instantly put Kathy at ease. He meandered around the common therapy room in blue scrubs and tennis shoes, frequently adjusting his glasses as they slipped down the bridge of his nose. His humor and the belly laugh shared with patients was infectious. You'd never guess the brilliance he embodied. Kathy recalls not being sure what to expect from this visit, but after a simple visual assessment of Conor, Doc was not intimidated by his deficits, nor was he lacking in confidence in his ability to help. There was no judgment or measurement of discouraging words. Rather, he simply said, "Let's get to work."

Functional neurology works off of the premise that the brain is plastic. In other words, the brain has the ability to rewire or reshape itself by sensory or motor input despite injury.[6] Functional neurology is non-invasive, which means change and improvement to impaired cerebral function is piloted through movement, which can reroute damaged neurons toward restoration and regeneration. "Brain damage," once considered permanent, in fact, didn't have to be. Doc offered hope and promise, and the Crippen orientation into the more extensive world of functional neurology was about to begin.

Doc took the time to explain how different parts of the brain work together, and how brain damage can be assessed by observation. The brain looks like a head of cauliflower sitting on a stick. The stick part is the brain stem, which connects all systems of the brain and nervous system and is the structural beginning of the spinal cord. The brain stem regulates breathing, heart rate, digestion, and other basic operations of the body. It made sense and we began to understand why, in the early days of Conor's recovery, those basic body function values were so erratic. The cerebellum sits just above the brain stem at the back of the head, overseeing operations like balance, coordination, and muscle movements. When injured due to trauma, the brain is torqued which can lead to diffuse neuron damage, which in Conor's case, affected even his brain stem. The continuum of healing needed

[6] "American College of Functional Neurology." *American College of Functional Neurology— Credentialing Functional Neurologist Since 2009*, acfn.org/.

to start from the base up in order to restore Conor's ability to control his center of gravity and stability. Once these basic functions were mastered, further healing was possible.

"He could stand and walk, so I knew he could do way better—WAY better," Doc recalled after seeing Conor for the first time. His hopeful approach picked up where Ann Anzalone left off. Although he saw expansive impairment in Conor's brain function, Doc's first challenge was to help Conor control his center of gravity and help him to stabilize his gaze. He explained that core strength is imperative. If a person isn't stable in his core, then maximum function of arms and legs is compromised.

Balance disorder, we came to learn, was an indicator of the severity of brain injury.[7] So with an exercise ball and enthusiasm rivaling a front row seat at the Super Bowl, Doc directed Conor to work on core exercises which would provide an anchor of strength as Conor expanded his capabilities. They forged a transcending relationship, connected not only by professional expertise and willingness to work, but also by a heart connection that reached far beyond Doc's therapy room. Grace was at work yet again, guided by the target: Conor's cerebellum.

. . . . .

My children attended the same public school where my sister taught. Stingley Elementary in Centerville, Ohio served students from kindergarten through fifth grade with educational intention and a nurturing environment. It was a close-knit school community where cohesiveness between teachers, parents, and students bred genuine regard. When success was generated, everyone joined in celebration. When tragedy affected one Stingley family, the entire school felt pain.

[7] Campbell, M. (2009). Balance Disorder and Traumatic Brain Injury: Preliminary Findings of a Multi-Factorial Observational Study. *Brain Injury, 19*(13), 1095–1104.

My children attended Stingley Elementary when news of a student's death sent vibrations of heartbreak through the local community. During a school winter break, we learned of a second-grade boy who had suffered a head injury while on a family ski trip and subsequently died. I recall my sister was so saddened by the news. She remembered him walking the art-decorated halls. This young and promising boy with a captivating smile was Conor's age, and the youngest of four children. Kathy could only imagine what his family was enduring. The "this could have been my child" possibility was haunting. The school built an outdoor memorial bench for him, just within reach of the playground where he once frolicked with his friends. His legacy remains within the giggles and playfulness of his school, even after all these years. His name was Charles Heuser, the son of Doc and Denise. During one of Conor's early appointments with him, Doc brought up Charles to my sister. This poetic verse of providence prompted reflection.

Remembering Charles with tenderness and sorrow, Kathy wondered if grace brought Conor and Doc together. We will never know if the chance encounter at DLM included some divine intention to heal not only Conor, but Doc and Denise as well. Brain trauma stole their bright and vibrant son, but perhaps they could bring the spirit of Charles with them as they committed to healing Conor. A stretch? Maybe. Then again, love was carving this path. I like to think Charles' spirit flourished between Doc and Conor. And just like the "MOTHER" sign that rotated off of Michigan Avenue, there was strength in believing those from above were propelling us in love. I've had many opportunities to watch Doc and Conor interact over the years, and I think of Charles often. I never knew him, but I know the gift of his life keeps on giving.

chapter 22

It's all about the eyes, Kathy would come to understand in a detailed and complex way. In his first appointment with Doc, Conor couldn't bring his gaze into fixation. Instead, when asked to look at something, Conor's gaze was jerky, exhibiting an increase in saccadic eye movements. "Saccade," the French word for "jerk," Doc explained, is a quick, simultaneous movement of both eyes, often signifying brain stem damage.[8] Unnoticeable to a layperson, Doc immediately picked up on Conor's saccadic eye movement, indicating the brain's inability to corral function. His explanation made sense. Focusing on one object requires a processing that says, "I want to pay attention to that," and then moves the eyes accordingly.

Through observation of subtle eye movement, Doc was able to gain clues indicating which parts of Conor's brain were functioning either too much or not enough. Eyes tracking a finger from right to left, or the finger-to-nose movement (like that done in a sobriety test), can indicate what exercises may be done to treat the brain's imbalance. The ability to keep the eyes focused takes significant computing power for two reasons. First, focusing on an object, Doc explained, requires the inhibition of all

---

[8] Mullen, Sarah J., et al. "Saccadic Eye Movements in Mild Traumatic Brain Injury: A Pilot Study OPEN ACCESS." *Canadian Journal of Neurological Sciences*, vol. 41, no. 01, 2014, pp. 58–65., doi:10.1017/s0317167100016279.

other activity. As the eye tracks a moving object, everything else surrounding that object "moves in" with it. Second, visual comprehension, which most of us take for granted, requires cooperation between the eyes (specifically, the retina) and the brain. Based on this clinical research, eye exercises can strengthen existing brain function and create new neural pathways.[9]

Doc recognized the severity of Conor's deficits but was certain of healing potential. He equated Conor's brain rehabilitation to peeling layers of an onion. One success will lead to the next. His approach was a game changer. He offered a plan that had no limit, and it really was quite simple: start with mastering the basics, like core strength to restore Conor's center of gravity and stabilize his gaze. Whereas other clinicians offered a protective prognosis, Doc realized that progress could not go farther than the expectations of the therapists' treatment.

Traditional neurologists are typically medical-school trained. Their charge is to diagnose, medicate, or refer patients to occupational or physical therapies. Conor's introduction to traditional neurology therapies at the RIC and follow-up treatments at OSU were instrumental in sparking his rebirth following the TBI. Certainly, we were grateful for medications to stimulate the brain and prevent seizures. Such treatments laid a groundwork for possibility and progress. Physical, speech, and occupational therapies were imperative in unlocking Conor's severely injured capacity to think or walk or talk or eat. Memories of various RIC therapists racking their professional brains to find some way to reach beyond Conor's injury still left us with immeasurable

[9] Peterson, Michelle D. "A Case-Oriented Approach Exploring the Relationship Between Visual and Vestibular Disturbances and Problems of Higher-Level Mobility in Persons With Traumatic Brain Injury." *Journal of Head Trauma Rehabilitation*, vol. 25, no. 3, 2010, pp. 193–205.

gratitude; but thereafter, Kathy and Phil reached a point where they wanted more for their son. As was the case with Conor's consultation in Chicago, suggestions to compensate for neurological deficits were frequently offered with, "he's just supposed to deal with it."

I asked Doc one time why functional neurology wasn't more respected and utilized in mainstream rehabilitation for TBI, especially given the amount of research supporting the premise. The more I learned and watched Conor improve, the more perplexed I became at the lack of functional neurologic practice in the mainstream world of brain rehabilitation. Shrugging his shoulders in agreement, all he could offer was a comparison of the two neurology paradigms; one based in traditional medical practice and the other in functional chiropractic paradigms.

Functional neurologists, on the other hand, are often chiropractic doctors trained in understanding the correlation between movement and improvement. For the Crippens, functional neurology picked up where traditional neurology left off. Trying new and innovative non-invasive treatments had no shortcoming. Doc explained that everything done in functional neurology has immediate assessment...*everything*. "So, if a patient's response isn't evident right then and there," he said, "that may not be the avenue you want to spend time on."

He was speaking encouraging language to my sister.

"If you can do something once, the brain is capable. If you can do it once, you can do it again. THAT," he continued, "is the TRUTH."

He went on to explain that the exercises to retrain the brain are doable, so that if you can fix one system of function—like ability to focus or balance—that can spill over to making subsequent improvements in brain function. With retraining, then, if Conor could bring his finger to his nose once without his right-arm tremor, he was capable of doing it again. Through repetition, success can be lasting.

Doc also reinforced the need for rest following therapies. The brain, after injury, is fragile and doesn't have the metabolic ability to process a signal for a sustained period of time. In the early stages following brain trauma, there's a fine balance between stimulating the brain and the ability to process new information. Rest is restorative: it provides an opportunity for the brain to oxygenate and refuel. If you drive brain activity without the opportunity to refuel, additional damage could be detrimental. The reminder was good for Kathy to hear, for Conor's healing did support "break times."

As Doc said, "The downside of doing eye exercises is so small, and the upside is very large. So, if the research supports it even a little bit, why not?" *Why Not?*

Doc's hope provided a lifeline. His philosophy for brain-injured people was that their future could be greater than ever anticipated, only if they are willing to do everything they need to in order to get there. "That's just the way it is," he said in his matter-of-fact way. You have to be fully committed, he reminded Kathy and Conor. The work is boring and there is often friction between the patient and the main coach. This was certainly the case for Kathy and Conor. Kitchen timers set for exercise sessions were, shall we say, annoying for him. Doc also mentioned that progress can be slow at times, and faster at times. It would be a long-range process.

"Ten years is going to go by one way or the other," he said. "You may as well make it about getting his life back. If you do something, it will be better in 10 years. If you don't, 10 years is going to go by one way or the other."

So began a professional relationship that rose to that place where grace lives. Doc's first impression of Kathy was that she was a force not to be reckoned with. He sensed her unyielding desire to help her son. He also instantly connected with Conor. These intangible foundations morphed into something greater, based in belief that divine providence brought them together, and that healing could be augmented by hope found in faith. Doc and Conor's philosophical connection bred a unique relationship. I heard Doc say once he loved Conor like a son. All roads to subsequent healing departed from this unassuming office with the sign **CHIROPRACTOR**. Doc and Denise would implant themselves deeply in this story of recovery. To this day, when Conor talks about Doc, it's usually preceded by a heavy sigh, then "Doc is amazing."

In my conversations with Doc long after his initial days with Conor, his articulation of his professional mission was informative and heartening. His hand-written flow charts explained how cerebral remapping can occur. Alongside his writing is my scribble, an attempt to further understand the research-based theories of functional neurology. With Doc, everything made more sense.

"The essence of humanity," he explained, "is the ability to extend and the ability to inhibit. But if a doctor ever says this is as good as it gets, then at that point trying ceases, then the current state becomes a self-fulfilling prophecy," he said.

This line, spoken with clarity, embodies the mission of this book. Conor's recovery continues—even years following his accident—because of Kathy and Phil's certainty that progress in healing is without limits, and because Doc said so. Kathy's dedication to bring Conor to wholeness could have been chalked up to mother's love or, perhaps, misguided optimism. Doc, however, gave definition to her love-driven purpose. He encouraged Kathy with his unbridled certainty that Conor could achieve full recovery and get his full life back. And about that right-hand tremor? Yup, Doc said, they could work on that.

After seeing Doc work with Conor for several years, I was curious as to why more people didn't buy into the unrelenting belief that healing from TBI was limitless. Doc shared his observations after years of treating those with such affliction. "Most people underestimate what can be done," he explained, "and more importantly, they underestimate what it takes to get there." Perhaps they are fatigued, or lack confidence, or have other things in their life preventing the full commitment to healing that brain retraining requires. The conventional wisdom of brain injury states "the prize isn't available," he told me. "There's an unwillingness to buy into the idea that the prize is out there if you work for it. If a patient won't do the work, it's because they aren't sold on the prize. There are belief systems that say, 'he can or can't be better.' Science says he can be better. And the fact is that very few people challenge traditional neurologists and therapists. So, for example, if a doctor says, 'You can never leave him alone,' no one challenges with, 'What research says that?'"

His words made perfect sense.

⚜ chapter 23 ⚜

Shortly after Conor's accident, Kathy's curiosity to learn of others' "victory stories" following brain injury led her to several books, including *In an Instant* by Bob and Lee Woodruff and *My Stroke of Insight* by Jill Bolte Taylor. Bob Woodruff, a correspondent for ABC News, was covering the war in Iraq when he suffered a critical brain injury from a roadside bomb. Jill Bolte Taylor, on the other hand, suffered brain trauma due to a stroke. While reading their chronicles of survival, we knew they recovered enough to lead productive, intuitive lives. They each wrote a book, after all. Although their history gave tangible hope for Conor, Kathy was left with the desire to know what their days would be like once they "survived" their injury. Certainly, they must have required intense therapy to help rewire their injured brain fibers, she thought, but where was the narrative regarding the daily commitment to regain high-functioning brain operation? Kathy wondered if their loved ones had the same bird's-eye view of therapy sessions that were painfully slow in progress, or showed no progress at all. She wondered if they needed to constantly recheck themselves in how much time this would take, or hope that a slight movement of a thumb would somehow connect to an unassisted walk around an outdoor track. Would life ever be ordinary again?

One Wednesday in September 2013, I sat with Conor during his therapy sessions at OSU where he was asked to identify red squares on a page that had shapes of all types and colors. It took him quite some time to point appropriately. Also at that time, his balance was still iffy, requiring support from someone at his side as he walked through his restless "breaks." His speech was but a whisper, and he only spoke in response to a question. Then, after several weeks of exercise repetition of the same concepts, Conor could identify the red squares and the yellow triangles without pause. He still needed to take his "breaks," but not as often and with less frequency. This defined progress, and we could see it best when we looked back to see how far he'd come.

As his speech therapist explained, there is a pyramid of cognitive function levels. At the bottom is simply the ability to focus, and then comes the ability to sequence and categorize. In the previous evaluation, Conor took 45 minutes to do his speech exercises. On this evaluation day, it took him less than five minutes to appropriately categorize shapes, animals, kitchen tools, or whatever else was placed before him. In physical therapy, Conor was able to balance on one leg while dribbling a basketball. And in occupational therapy, an exercise that he could not even complete the month before, he was able to perform completely in just a few minutes. These examples are short of the breakthrough advances in recovery, but TBI rehab is not about breakthroughs. It is about finding comfort in knowing each month has the potential to be better than the last.

Kathy and Phil knew success came in small increments. Lining pegs on a pegboard, prompting short term memory, or repeating a sequence of actions with intention were among the various therapeutic exercises designed to restore brain function. This was the world of rehabilitation. There was no quick fix, however Conor embodied confidence just like he always had. He exuded optimism despite the challenges of his personal renovation. He kept my sister lifted by his humor and willingness to do whatever it took to get better. Conor showed her every day what it meant to keep the faith.

As Conor gained more insights regarding the impact of his accident, he began to ask more questions. He was curious about the doctors, nurses, and therapists who worked tirelessly to save his life. Brain trauma wiped years of memory from his consciousness, and the only connection he had to the extraordinary efforts to save him were through the stories told by those who sat by his side. Some accounts became iconic, like the surgical procedure that resulted in his skull flaps being placed in his belly for two months. He laughed when Kathy recounted the numerous therapy sessions when Conor's stubbornness literally prevented "one foot in front of the other." Respect and affection for his caregivers and therapists became known through his family's gratitude. And when Phil replayed the video of Conor taking the steps of their home staircase two at a time just days after his homecoming, Conor simply replied, "Well, that's how I always do stairs."

There was one memory, however, that Conor was very clear about and was his alone. Sometime between the night of the accident and when his ability to communicate returned, Conor experienced and encounter with someone named Thomas. The where and when are hazy, but according to Conor, there was no doubt about the who. The voice was clear and Conor heard it loud and strong.

"Conor, my name is Thomas, and you WILL be OK."

The proclamation of confidence provided an overwhelming feeling of comfort and gave Conor hope by reaffirming his resilience. Yet, by all recorded accounts, there was no one by the name of Thomas who interacted with Conor at any time during his critical care. After learning about Thomas, Kathy and Phil searched through all medical reports. No first responders, no emergency personnel, and no hospital personnel by that name were associated with Conor's care.

Was this one of those "near death" experiences where Conor was "visited" by some heavenly being? Conor would tell you that's not up to him to decide. I asked him once if he thought Thomas was God or some representative of heaven. He replied he didn't know, but that Thomas' aura was pure and all-encompassing. We talked about how the experience of his supernatural meeting may have set the tone for Conor's calm and centered demeanor throughout his lengthy recovery process, but I wanted to know more.

I asked Conor what Thomas looked like, to which he responded, "I just saw his face and was mesmerized by his voice."

When I tried to push Conor to add physical features to Thomas, he pushed back.

"Everyone wants to physicalize him, and I can't. I'm not going to skew the lens or use him as a marketing tool to plug spiritual agendas. My experience can't be thrust on everyone. Thomas was a possibility that just happened, but it was the closest thing to nirvana I've ever experienced. I trusted him. Thomas was life, and he gave me more comfort than anyone ever. He just was."

I wondered if there was any connection between Conor's Thomas and my brother Thomas who died at birth. I know it was a stretch, but who am I to limit heavenly possibilities? When I brought up to Conor that perhaps it was my brother Thomas, he laughed. He reminded me that his "uncle" Thomas was never really on his radar even prior to the accident.

Conor recognized my tendencies to stretch his account so that I could attach more sense or meaning to his story, and remained patient as I tried to place his story into the category of "where heaven meets earth." Conor, however, shrugged his shoulders. His takeaway was simple: gratitude.

Thomas became a friend like no other somewhere between accident impact and consciousness, which for us was a long time. He touched a spiritual place in Conor and left a legacy of confidence and revelation that all would be well. Maybe it was Thomas, after all, that serenaded the sweet song of life into Conor's spirit during those days when all we heard was the beeping of life support. Perhaps this interaction laid the seeds for Conor's remarkable acceptance of his accident. The rest of us will never know, but Conor does. Thomas just was.

As we approached the six-month mark since Conor's accident, perspective was a gift. Kathy and Phil were now able to look back and reflect on how far Conor had come. His recovery defied the odds, considering his initial Glasgow Coma Score of 3. Given the gift of survival, the Crippens were empowered by the future; looking forward with hope. The now, however, was laced with gift of living in the ordinary amidst the extraordinary. Kathy navigated Conor's non-negotiable schedule of tutoring, yoga, massage, acupuncture, and sessions with Doc and Ann Anzalone, yet the mundane was now possible. Simple experiences like lunch at Chipotle or witnessing brother-banter with Jack reminded her that Conor was improving and that the journey toward wellness was in place. What we had also come to realize was that we were not the only inhabitants who found our way out of the vacuum of heartache. The constant awareness of so many who suffered unimaginable pain or loss provided daily opportunities for humility and pause.

August 26, 2013 PRFC

As I was driving to work this morning, I was privy to the sun rising, which quickly brought the light of day. I have to honestly admit I am not an early morning person, and if it were not for my early work shift, I would have surely missed the dramatic show of the sun bursting forth. While subconsciously driving in my car, I shifted my glance and was absolutely awed by the brilliant, fiery, and intense entrance of our sun. It was huge! I thought, almost whimsically, that the sun I saw this morning had just left the other half of the world, but still had the intense and fervent brightness to share with us as it did with those it had just left. And so it goes, right?…every day, no less. I was humbled.

As life continues for Conor and his family, the trend toward healing continues. Each day brings progress; the pace is slow but steadfast. Reworking an injured brain just takes time. Time is on our side, and we know that now. I learned today of another young woman in Ann Arbor, Michigan who was hit by a car while riding her bike and suffered a severe brain injury. Her name is Angela, and she is currently fighting for her life. Our hearts connect with her family. Most probably, her mom and dad are at her bedside looking at monitors, holding her hand willing some kind of connection, and praying harder than they have ever prayed before. And then there is Conor's old neighbor from the RIC. Just a few rooms down was Lauren Murphy, a promising and beautiful young woman hit by a car while jogging in the early morning of a routine work day. After many months of rehabilitation in Chicago, she returned home this past weekend. We hope and pray that she will have the same progress in recovery that Conor has had since being home.

There are so many stages in this marathon of TBI, or any other of life's incomprehensible tragedies. All I know is that our collective sun rose brilliantly today. Of course, as I witnessed the stunning brightness and display of life-giving reds and oranges this morning, I immediately, by default, saw this as a sign for my sister, her family, and for Conor. As they begin this week, all of the Crippens need to rearm themselves with the resolve and grounded faith that have sustained them, but sometimes need a bit of tweaking. And then I thought of Lauren and Angela, and all those whose names we don't even know. That bright sun that I saw this morning make such a grand entrance to my world is the same bright sun that I pray will illuminate the day for all those who so desperately need some light. For those who desperately connect one moment to the next feeling smothered by despair, we pray for healing and the awareness that God is indeed present. For those who are crafting (hopefully) opportunities for ordinary time at home, we pray that they will see the blessings before them. We are all, after all, under the light of one sun. It shines for all.

Conor's hard work to restore higher-level brain function was slow and tedious. Daily reminders that healing had no limit were plastered all over the Crippen house. Kathy loved words, and those that inspired were stenciled on the walls. Messages on the miniature chalkboard in their kitchen narrated the call to inspire. Conor was going to get better, one grueling day at a time. Kathy's signature chalk handwriting left no room for doubt. Each day offered a new message.

"Tiny tweaks lead to big changes!"

As Conor embarked on the painstaking, dull litany of exercises to attain greater cognitive function, his mom's words resonated.

"Awesome ain't easy!"

Between protein-packed kale smoothies and the mental taxation of recalling how to make instant oatmeal, Kathy's reminders provided constant encouragement.

"Be realistic, expect a miracle."

The vast world of rehabilitation was overwhelming, but that didn't stop Kathy from disarming the challenge with simple daily thoughts.

**"For I know the plans I have for you, declares the Lord,
plans to prosper you and not harm you,
plans to give you hope and a future." Jeremiah 29:11**

The mission was relentless, and there would be no settling for anything other than Conor's full capability to live a productive and independent life.

Several months following Conor's accident, I was invited to join Kathy and Conor at a prayer service for his healing. Three members from Incarnation Catholic Church in Dayton had invited Kathy and Conor to join them for an intimate prayer session; their ministry sought to connect earthly needs with divine intervention. It was a simple gathering. We turned the chairs in the small chapel to make a circle. The mood and environment whispered simplicity. There were merely three people who brought themselves with the confidence that God, indeed, was available to help just because they were asking.

Again, I had a front row seat to the grace of God. The sharing of their time to embolden Kathy and Conor with prayer left me humbled. They touched Conor with tenderness, and they were so sure of the heavenly presence surrounding him. I was moved that they cared so deeply and hoped so surely for this young man they had never met. And they believed wholeheartedly that prayer works and God listens.

I was also moved by their gentle attention to my sister. That day, Kathy wore the fatigue and desire for Conor's healing in the dark rings under her eyes and deepening lines on her face. Her eyes shed the tears that had been building as she spent her days in complete dedication to the mission. She was "seen" by these generous-hearted people. The softness of their eyes met hers. The strength of their touch as they rested their hands on her shoulders represented the poetic faith of God showing up through others.

Prior to Conor's accident, I was a bit skeptical regarding the ability for prayer to affect outcome. Those stories of miraculous disappearance of cancer or inexplicable ability to walk despite paralysis left me dubious. But then we found ourselves in the throes of desperation; all we had was prayer. This was different from the finality of Neil and Pat's lives. Prayer wouldn't have changed their death. But Conor survived, and in those early hours following his accident, we fell to our knees in humility. We needed God and any healing interventions the great world of grace could provide. And then a community of supporters showed up within hours of our first Facebook post. They, too, believed that prayer could heal. The extension of others felt like a warm blanket on a cold winter's night. Prayer kept the Crippens connected to hope, and hope propelled Kathy's ability to navigate the road to recovery.

Did prayer actually help Conor improve? I guess you could make an argument either way, but I learned through observing my sister's journey that resting in the power of prayer yielded strength and optimism. *Why not?* Love, after all, heals every time. And the fact was, Conor defied all odds.

We were keenly aware of his progress, yet we knew there was still a long way to go. Angst was the permanent guest that accompanied this journey. Being with Conor, however, unplugged us from life's clutter. His beauty, his gentleness, his ability to love, and his now-famous hug made us truly feel as if we were enveloped in the symphony of grace.

So, here's to prayer. The humility of lifting your hand to say, *I'm raising the white flag,* is a good thing. It means you open yourself to the power that others can provide through their own faith that transcends doubtfulness. As Kathy moved from day to day, the path forward wasn't always visible through the fog of doubt. Despite the inclination to coil amidst her ache, Kathy remained open and was willing to try anything that offered the potential for healing movement. If one avenue didn't work, she kept looking for another. The process was exhausting. Times like this, when I saw others lift her spirit through prayer, I was grateful.

✦ chapter 24 ✦

They say we take out our frustrations on those we love the most. It's not unusual for brothers to pick on or exacerbate emotional irritations with each other. I recall having to separate my own two boys during their shared years at home due to overreacting scuffle. Although such tendencies are normal, in the months following Conor's accident, his rebirth included consistent impatience with Jack. As Conor navigated his own aggravations in reconciling his brain injury, Jack could do nothing right. Conor was often argumentative and sarcastic with Jack, and although the prickly sentiments came and went quickly, there was a period of months where Jack absorbed the brunt of Conor's annoyances. The criticisms expressed by Conor to his brother felt, at times, like a pounding of negativity. We all knew this was a byproduct of Conor's own exasperations, but Jack took it all in stride. Not once did he retaliate with spicy words or challenge, even though Conor's verbal outbursts were without warrant. Not once. The patience, compassion, and loyalty Jack exhibited were remarkable. He gave new definition to the role of "my brother's keeper."

If you would ask anyone involved in the Crippen story who the real hero was during this very prolonged saga of recovery, hands down, the answer would be Jack. From the age of 16 when Conor was severely injured, Jack stepped up with steadfast understanding and wisdom regarding the needs of his family, and in particular, his brother. While Conor and Kathy spent months in Chicago, Jack was left home alone days at a time during his most formative years of high school. Phil had a suitcase constantly packed as he commuted from home. All energy was dedicated to Conor's recovery. Jack could have taken advantage of the opportunity to engage in "independent" behavior or shirk his academic responsibilities due to the profound shift in family priority. It would have been understandable if Jack harbored resentment or allowed typical teenaged self-centeredness to jade his perspective on the altered course of family priority. Remarkably, his response to their collective strain was to focus on his responsibilities so that his parents wouldn't have to bear additional worry. He studied, he showed up to track meets, and he found a way to not need much from anyone. Kathy and Phil were well aware of the enormity of Jack's self-responsibility, but they had no other choice than to depend on him to do forge ahead, often on his own. Their second son's rise in unassuming strength and commitment to family was astonishing.

As 2013 came to a close, Kathy and Phil continued to navigate Conor's recovery; utilizing every means in their power, they gave thanks for ordinary time. For uneventful Sunday dinners, for restoration of Conor's smile and humor, and for the team of therapists, educators, and healers. Just a few months prior, the wish to engage in a family dinner around the Crippen kitchen table was but a desperate hope.

With the holidays approaching, I was keenly aware of the difference one or even two years makes. My gratitude stretched far beyond anything we could have imagined one year earlier. Prior to the gathering of family, I reflected. I think you could call this a love letter to all those who cared enough to stand with us.

November 23, 2013 PRFC

There is a quiet to this Saturday morning. The grocery list for children coming home and Thanksgiving dinner is growing in my mind, but not yet written. There is a pause before the hustle and bustle. Lately, Kathy and I have talked of the pending holiday season, and again, this year's gathering will mark the unexpected events that our family brings with us to the table. Last year, in my journaling, I wrote of the loss of my mom and my brother, Neil. The bravery we needed then to show up despite the huge void in our hearts was tangible. Yet as a family, we did only what we have always known: we gathered with open arms and supportive hearts. The aware-ness then was to fill the void of loss with love, remembrance, and gratitude for one another.

This year feels quite different. Although our hearts still yearn for a mom and a larger-than-life brother, we are all quite aware that if but for an instant (and the incredible intervention by those at Advocate Illinois Masonic Hospital), we could have been in an even deeper abyss of loss. Because of the grace of an entire system of God's touch, we gather this year in celebration for the life of Conor.

Last night, we welcomed our Matthew (my son), who had not been home in several months. Conor and the Crippens stopped by to see him. Matthew had not had the opportu-nity to have simple time with his cousin since the summer, and as we stood around our kitchen smiling, toasting, and delighting in Conor's laughter, we all noted the presence of the extraordinary in the ordinary. The ability to gather care-free, once again, felt as if our cups were overflowing with a heightened mindfulness of gratitude. As Conor and Matthew stood back to back to see who is taller (because Conor seems to have grown in height since March), the strength of Conor's legs allowing him to stand tall, the beauty of his hair now grown following his life-saving cranial surgeries, the smile at knowing he trumps his cousin in height, and his capacity to be "in the game" of conversation, ability to listen, and growth in awareness of his place within our great family were all duly noted. Such things we will never take for granted.

You have all been such an important part in this journey. Your words of encouragement, belief, and determined hope provided a multitude of light rays when despair tempted the company of fear for the Crippens. Those first weeks of blind faith following Conor's accident were bearable, in large part, due to your companionship. There is so much to reflect upon as we begin the week of Thanksgiving. The visual of Kathy and Bridget—in the SICU with phones in hand reading your words posted throughout those early days—helped them to literally move from one worry moment to the next. Your cards, your gifts, your photos, and your unrelenting hope have left the ability to say that good has trumped the awfulness of Conor's accident. We have not forgotten, nor will we ever forget, how sustaining your support has been.

The work to restore Conor fully is well in place. Our confidence has grown, and we now include those on our Go Conor Go team in our hearts of gratefulness. They believe as we do: that Conor will get back to the business of realizing all God calls him to be. I will probably repeat myself a few more times as we move through these next weeks, but if my mom were here, she would say that one cannot say "thank you" enough. I raise my coffee cup to you all. Go Conor Go!

Family trickled from near and far, and I wondered how we could encapsulate our joy. Gathering around one very long table to share our traditional Thanksgiving meal was nothing short of a miracle. Yet the poetic flow of the day was extraordinarily wrapped up in the beauty of the ordinary.

We followed our usual family tradition. One by one, we went around the table and said what we were thankful for. Grogans tend to linger a bit in taking time to measure the year with grateful words. Allowing everyone their turn to give thanks is really a course of its own and certainly not for the "eat-and-run" kind of person. Beautiful sentiments were expressed and tears of gratitude flowed simply because Conor sat in his place, nestled among his siblings and cousins. Their "kid" end of the table was historically where the unruly gathered, and the fact that this year, once again, our collective children were laughing together, high-fiving each other, and teasing one another was perhaps the most beautiful component of the day. The wholeness of having them all together was precious. Conor sat among his cousins. Looking at him you would never know how close we all were in losing him. Bridget wept openly in gratitude. And Jack...well, he'd already garnered the kind of respect from his extended family one could only hope to achieve in a lifetime. We'd all been watching him and admiring his selflessness. To this day, Jack remains our hero.

My daughter Kate shared the most notable comment. She spoke of the ways we redefined ourselves. Our ability to "show up" for one another stretched well beyond our previous capabilities. The daily and sometimes hourly choice to believe and rest in hope was now a fortress amidst life's challenges. Kathy and Phil's love for their son surpassed any previous call to parenthood. The sadness and despair of our family story from one year ago morphed into a narrative of triumph expanding each day. And the quintessential redefinition is that our Conor continued to heal. As the Crippens posed for a family photo, you would have never known such a tragic accident happened. But it did. Ordinary holiness was met with the mindfulness that this Thanksgiving could have been despairingly different. But instead, my sister, through her courageous example, broadened the scope of survival to include honesty, gratitude, creativity and love. Grounded in grace, Kathy persisted.

from the ashes, new life

⤳ chapter 25 ⤳

January 2014

Because of her ability to focus exclusively on Conor's recovery, Kathy's search continued to have no boundaries. She was approachable to anything or anyone that offered a chance for improvement. As long as there was no potential for harm, every avenue was explored. Still on the weekly schedule were acupuncture, yoga, and massage therapy, as well as traditional physical, speech, and occupational therapies. My sister's broad definition of how spiritual energies coexist in our vast universe left her receptive in believing that healing power came in all ways and from all places. Born from the days when Kathy would accompany my mom to psychics in search of clarity regarding the heavenly well-being of Pat or longing to know more about her biological birth parents instilled a mystical open-mindedness.

Every time I spoke to her, it seemed she was on the trail of discovery for alternative therapies. You never knew where a full tank of gas would take Kathy and Conor any given week. When a friend recommended a chiropractor in Pittsburgh who apparently worked wonders, they went. When another mother of a disabled child referred Kathy to a healer in Cleveland who positively impacted her son, they went. Nothing was off the table. She read books, listened to podcasts, watched TED talks, and researched creative ways to help Conor's brain heal. Nutritional supplements to enhance brain function were lined up on her kitchen counter. Refined sugars were eliminated from his diet. The enhancement of physical endurance was closely balanced with down-time, whereby giving his brain ample intervals to rest. Intention defined everything.

For the most part, however, Conor's therapeutic unearthing was done at home. The challenge to make new brain connections came in all kinds of ways, and as they moved further and further away from acute concerns, the challenge of problem solving became more daring. Take, for example, Conor's first experience with rock climbing.

Why not? They thought as Phil took Conor to the community recreation center for a Saturday morning rock-climbing class. The echoes of professional suggestions that Conor would never be able to think in high-functioning ways were muffled by Phil's "wows" as Conor navigated the climbing wall. It was that cross-crawl movement again that Ann Anzalone advocated. Conor securely placed a hand, then assessed where to place the opposite foot; and then he did it again, working his way up the climbing wall. The harness supporting Conor's body provided peace of mind, and his climb took time, but eventually the ability to strategically place one hand then one foot on the modular holds left Phil in amazement. After several practice sessions, the collective cheer among his audience of Saturday morning rec center attendees rose to the rafters as he rang the bell at the top. Conor turned to mush the "expert" predictions once again.

Maintaining a state of exploration was exhausting. I knew my sister's emotional state at "hello," and could instantly tell when weariness exposed her fears. Her tendency to become discouraged coincided with her sense that current interventions felt like they were running their course. Wanting more and finding ways to get there generated impatience and urgency. I loved my sister with the surest love I've ever known, and my powerlessness to make things easier for her left me heavy with a sadness I had to bury somewhere beneath my façade of stability and stout encouragement. Kathy's collapse into her own grief and trepidation didn't happen often, but when it did, the flush of pent up tears left my heart broken yet again. When she was called to new definitions of patience in hopes for Conor to move to a next phase of healing, I saw it in her eyes. When she wished nothing more than to crawl into her bed from fatigue, I saw her stretch her arms and reposition her shoulders so that somehow, somewhere, new energy would emerge.

Because I was in the unique position of watching my sister, I knew someday Kathy's daily life would not be dictated by this challenge; but to tell her that while she crafted each day with intention and hope might have made her want to throw a pie in my face. When she felt depleted, I had to choose my words carefully. When down and out, there's nothing worse than someone trying too hard to encapsulate misfortune with shallow words. I knew how that felt.

Through my writing, I was privy to the correlation between the Crippen situation and others who found themselves in unimaginable heartache. So many people reached out to us through Conor's Facebook page, sharing their stories and offering encouragement. The challenge of bringing light to a vast continuum of darkness was not my sister's challenge alone. Yes, the complicated aftermath of traumatic brain injury is unique and not easily understood by others who've never known the ill-defined road to recovery, but that didn't mean there wasn't a vast opportunity to share the meaning of survival.

I came to know a local woman, Marianne, who was battling metastatic cancer. Although her journey and my sister's journey were quite different, we were able to connect, in part because of uninvited hurdles. Learning how to reset yourself in the midst of tribulation, resisting the temptation to define yourself by broken-ness, and recognizing the language of grace were all things we shared. We decided to meet for coffee.

I sat across from Marianne and saw in her eyes what it means to be real. The wisps of newly grown hair were evidence of her fight for life. The twinkle of her eyes and the brilliance of her smile offered proof of her resistance in being defined by her unwelcome journey. We talked about the shock of her diagnosis so many years ago, and the persistence she's had in battling her metastatic disease. Her eyes communicated compassion and love as we shared the blessings each of us have experienced through heartache. The ability to express joy despite her pain reminded me of my mom. I knew the time would come when Kathy would offer her own outreach for others who carried unanticipated burdens, but she wasn't there yet. She was still in the throes of her streamlined mission.

Avoiding the possibility of pie in my face, sometimes I would try and reach my sister through my written word.

February 3, 2014 PRFC

Last week, I was fortunate enough to attend a writer's workshop at a retreat venue called Kripalu, nestled in the Berkshires in western Massachusetts. Grace led me to this place where I would share five days with strangers who also came to write. We bonded quickly. Sitting in the circle on the floor in an open room, writing from the heart, and allowing vulnerabilities to be exposed facilitated the written word to paint our life portrait. It did not take long to get to know their souls. It took even less time to adore them.

I listened in awe as my fellow writers read their stories of storm survival, traumatic violence, love-starved beginnings, and the need to flee their homeland. Their poetic words wove threads of beauty into their suffering. Without fail, as each of us shared chapters from our lives, we were met with soft eyes of empathy and compassionate ears of understanding. All of us somehow had the universal knowing of what it means to survive. We laughed and we cried together.

Upon leaving Kripalu, I called my sister with overwhelming emotion. I wanted to communicate to her what I had been reminded of after being with such gifted writers. The journey is the triumph, and the road of humanity has more to share than we realize. The road is what connects. Whether we call it grace or not, somehow, we must weave one moment to the next in adversity. I have been witness to the all-consuming struggle and challenge that has been so keenly a part of Conor's healing. I also know that my sister walks every step of every day with intention and creativity facilitating Conor's recovery. My writing friends reminded me that in time, the life force of this chapter of Conor's story will lessen, and the ability to create a different life will grow. It is not forever that we will be "living in" the aftermath of Conor's accident. There will be a time when we will "bring with" his story to a greater tapestry. And there will be a day when Conor, in particular, will bless the world with infinite possibility.

Last week, I literally stepped out into the bigger world "bringing with" love for my sister, hope for Conor, and trust in his healing journey. I was met with expanded air where I could inhale a grand and universal love, and exhale a knowing that we really are being supported by a world of grace greater than we even know. I see my sister as the best version of herself, but I know how focused she remains. Those who I came to know helped me to understand that when my sister feels like she can relax into life again, when her breath expands, she will "bring with" her story that will inspire and empower others. My Kripalu friends were living proof to the testament of survival in life's continuum. Their wounds have healed, and their scars add to their beauty. They are no longer in that place.

And so, I rest in the rhythm of breath, the inhale and the exhale that we all take for granted, but propels us from one life giving moment to the next. What a journey we are all on, and what stories we all have to share. Be aware of your breath, I learned. There is purpose and beauty even in the unknown. With gratitude to all who imprinted my heart last week. Go Conor Go!

Recovery from brain injury takes years. There is no quick fix. Kathy could have never processed the extent of the commitment in the immediate aftermath of Conor's accident, but in time, she learned the key to success was patience and open-mindedness. In her words, the perspective is that of stepping stones, one in front of the other. With her piqued curiosity, acute senses, and willingness to be bold, Kathy pursued every possibility. The path of healing for Conor was not linear. Rather, opportunities to help him came about because Kathy's eyes and ears were constantly seeking therapeutic prospects that came about because one stone led to another.

Doc continued to be a steady participant in Conor's therapy regime. His practical encouragement regarding the brain's plasticity and ability to heal continued to provide tangible hope. Doc referred Conor to a former colleague, Dr. Frederick (Ted) Carrick in Atlanta. A Neuro-chiropractor, Dr. Carrick founded the Carrick Institute for Clinical Neuroscience and Rehabilitation. His Plasticity Brain Centers are the go-to rehabilitation facility for professional hockey players, snowboarders, and football players who suffer from traumatic brain injuries. Reactivating neurological pathways in the brain through stimulation of various parts of the body was the same clinical message Kathy heard from Doc. Overnight bag in tow, Kathy and Conor set off for Atlanta (Dr. Carrick's former clinic location).

For my sister, the most critical component in evaluating therapists was whether or not these people believed in Conor's capacity to improve. The Carrick team did from the outset. The research-supported matter-of-fact confidence offered by Doc was the same opinion offered by the Atlanta team. Reactivating brain pathways by stimulating parts of the body could improve brain function. Following a week-long treatment program, Conor came home with a daily exercise regime and an appointment to return to in a few months for reevaluation. Kathy felt emboldened by the combination of new therapists on board. The view from the road was wide open. The ensuing weeks and months of intensive home therapy combined with Conor's increasing desire for independence spoke to Kathy and Phil. It was time to take a chance.

☙ chapter 26 ☙

In January 2015, the decision was made that Conor would return to Loyola University for the spring semester. Phil, too, would commit to a short-term Chicago residency for support. Excited to resume all aspects of college life, Conor moved into a house near Wrigley Field where his friends Casey and Keenan had a vacant bedroom waiting. Hanging out with roommates, ordering late-night chicken wings, and supplying backpacks with text books and highlighters constituted some of the happenings of college life Conor longed to resume. In his mind, he was still accountable to the stolen exam week imminently scheduled just days after his accident. Kathy and Phil understood the longing, and set out to do whatever it took to get Conor to pick up where he left off in life.

Phil was fortunate enough to have the capability to work remotely from Chicago where he rented a month-by-month leased apartment just blocks from where Conor lived. Move in day was a family affair. Kathy and Bridget applied labels to all of the cabinets and drawers in Conor's kitchen reminding him of where the silverware, cereal, and aluminum foil were located. Loss of short-term memory really puts a crimp into retaining useful information, like where the spatula is to flip a grilled cheese sandwich. Practical living for Conor required a multitude of cues. Phil accompanied Conor on a few trial runs to campus so that Conor could remember when and where his classes were located. Reminders of daily schedules were hung in Conor's bedroom. The most important tool in navigating daily life was his cell phone. Conor would be in constant contact with his mom or dad, navigating, negotiating and problem-solving his way to independent life. Not only that, the smartphone calendar and timers reminded Conor to eat, sleep and take his anti-seizure medication. All of this and Phil's heavy participation in Conor's class requirements continued to thread the needle toward the academic success Conor experienced prior to his accident. This, after all, was his destiny—whatever it took.

Phil often jokes that when Conor went back to school, so did he. Although Conor had the professor's permission to tape his classes for review, it was Phil who created study guides and—shall we say—"helped" with the assignments. Conor's understanding of the relationship between atoms and molecules was as sharp as ever. If academic success could have been measured by oral argument, Conor's abilities would have been a slam dunk. It was all the other components required for academic success—organizing class notes, retaining information for test taking, and balancing the need to rest an overtaxed brain—that became factors in the challenge. At the end of the semester, the consensus was, it was too soon to resume life in Chicago. Conor wasn't ready. There was still healing work to do.

Conor came home in May 2015 with renewed goals to build independence and continue healing. The transition was difficult for him, however, as the desire for independent life felt stalled. For any college kid, coming home after living away is sometimes tough. Kathy and Phil, too, felt troubled by the unknown. Phil wrote:

August 2, 2015 PRFC

Even though it was great to be home, it was a major transition time for us all. Since Conor's accident, we always knew the next step or had a goal in mind. Even though Conor made progress in Chicago, we realized he was not ready to live independently at this time, so the dream of him going back this fall needed to be postponed.

Once we had to readjust our goals, we started to question what that would be and even if we have been doing the right things all along. Were we doing the right therapies? Were we pushing him too hard? Not enough? Doubt and fear start to creep in and complicate the process of thinking clearly. For Kathy and I especially the first 30 days back home were challenging. Thankfully, like we've experienced in this entire journey, God slowly revealed the next steps for Conor.

Conor began volunteering in Mark's office and became an ambassador for cancer patients who were on a different quest for healing, but required the same tenacity Conor embodied. He took some online classes, continued with "Carrick exercises," and was given the medical go ahead to begin driving. Doc offered Conor a job in his office, where working with brain injured and stroke patients could offer an opportunity for Conor to offer help to those who suffered from various forms of brain injury. His testimonial in sharing his personal story provided infectious gave hope and encouragement. Doc also used the opportunity to continue with informal therapy sessions. Their relationship moved to a level of deeper mutual admiration.

It was about this time Kathy received an email from Amazon. com "suggesting" a book based on her previous "searches." As we all do, Kathy deleted most spam-like emails without bothering to open them, but this time something caught her eye. A book entitled *The Ghost in My Brain* was written by a professor at DePaul University in Chicago. After suffering debilitating consequences due to a concussion, Clark Elliott, Ph.D. found himself frustrated following eight years of being told he couldn't fully recover. In his book he writes,

> One of the things concussives share is the feeling of having become an alien being. We still walk and talk and act as though we are part of the human race, but it doesn't feel that way inside. Essential parts of our brains convey what it means to be fully humans have disappeared—vanished in that moment of impact when we tripped on the stairs, or crashed into an area wall. Instead there is a strange feeling of nostalgia, a longing for who we used to be.
>
> *Normals*—those who haven't suffered from concussions—will take for granted the countless small operations their brains perform as they think and gracefully move their bodies through the day. But a concussive loses the ability to manage the staggering complexity of the systems that implement these operations, and as a result loses not only basic cognitive and motor function but also a larger sense of self-identity and identity in relation to the world.[10]

Dr. Elliott, too, was professionally advised to "deal with" his symptoms and "learn to live with them."

Like Kathy, Dr. Elliott was not satisfied with limited recovery. In his quest to find something beyond traditional therapies, Dr. Elliott learned of Donalee Markus, Ph.D. and Deborah Zelinsky, O.D. whose research was based in brain injury and methods of

---

[10] *"The Ghost in My Brain: How a Concussion Stole My Life and How the New Science of Brain Plasticity Helped Me Get It Back*, by Clark Elliott, Penguin Books, 2016, pp. 22–23.

rehabilitation. Dr. Markus uses puzzles to restructure cognitive function, and Dr. Zelinsky targets rewiring of the brain through custom-made therapeutic eyeglass lenses. After reading Dr. Elliott's book, Kathy called Dr. Markus, made an appointment, and within days she and Conor were on the road again to Chicago. Both Dr. Markus and Dr. Zelinsky would work with Conor for the ensuing months, helping him to restore cognitive function which translated to practical abilities in the greater world.

The next year was designed to get Conor back to Loyola, once again, to pursue his academic goals. Perhaps it was a narrow definition, but full recovery for Conor meant he would continue his pre-accident goal of attaining a college degree. By August 2016, Kathy and Phil felt Conor was ready to take the plunge, this time by himself. They helped move him into an apartment just across the street from Loyola's campus. Close proximity to classroom venues would alleviate the challenges of navigating the complex Chicago public transportation system. Initially, the study of chemistry and science felt overwhelming, so Conor turned his focus to the study of philosophy. Discussions regarding Buddhism and existential purpose were easy for him, and fed his innate quest to search for life's meaning. His propensity for spiritual learning never waned, and the chance to discuss knowledge of the enlightened was stimulating.

For the next nine months, Conor remained eager to learn and expand his academic mind. The problem was still the logistics. The volume of reading assignments, paper writing, and comprehensive study requirements for exams eventually took their toll. His short-term memory deficits continued to be an obstacle. By spring 2017 Conor was exhausted. Perhaps the backup batteries that Clark Elliott describes in *Ghost in My Brain* made sense. In his book, Elliott writes:

Imagine that a concussive has three sets of batteries that power her brain. Set A—the working set—is immediately available, and also recharges rapidly within a few hours. Set B—the first level of backup batteries—can be accessed if Set A is exhausted, but takes longer to recharge, possibly up to several days. Set C—the deepest level of backup batteries—can be used as a last resort at times of extreme demand when Set B is exhausted. But caution must be exercised—Set C charges very slowly, over the course of up to two weeks.

As long as our concussive can get by using her Set A batteries to power her brain, life will be relatively normal. But this means that her brain can only be used for short periods, and not in ways that are very demanding. The concussive needs periods of doing nothing, without thinking, or dreaming, or taking action.[11]

In hindsight, the push to return to academia was too much. Yes, Conor was living independently in Chicago, and yes, he was taking classes. In the realm of status quo measured by appearance, he had returned to "normal" living, but he was not thriving. Rather, he was sinking from an over taxation of his brain energy. He suffered from perpetual depletion. Kathy and Phil were challenged with helping to manage the situation from afar and spoke to Conor by phone hourly if not more helping him to navigate school work, logistics, and the connection of one hour to the next. Despite the appearance of normalcy, the demands of maintaining an academic life were still too draining. He was literally exhausted with no battery power left.

Reality, however, eventually teaches us, and after two years of

[11] "The Human Machine Is Broken." The Ghost in My Brain: How a Concussion Stole My Life and How the New Science of Brain Plasticity Helped Me Get It Back, by Clark Elliott, Penguin Books, 2016, pp. 57–59.

trying to make an academic comeback work, the three Crippens realized it just wasn't working. The signs of distress grew as winter turned to spring. Fearing Conor's academic load would come to do more harm than good to his mending brain, Kathy and Phil agreed he needed to come home…immediately. In their minds, pushing him to stay even one more week to finish the term was too much.

Finally, clarity set in. Conor's new chance at life didn't have to fit into his former goals. The dogged aim to resume his academic quest was too draining. It was time to bring him home and reevaluate short term goals. Kathy and Phil felt an urgency to release the sustained pressure Conor was under. Once the mutual decision was made, Phil was on the road to Chicago once again. He returned 24 hours later; a worn-out Conor in tow. They would send in his final assignments via email. The Crippens looked forward to creating some restful space for Conor where new ideas for his future and inspiration regarding his life mission would emerge. Any disappointment that Conor didn't finish the semester was short-lived. It would simply be enough to have him home and settle into some ordinary time. The reality, though, was "ordinary" would not be a luxury for any Crippen for quite some time. Unbeknownst to this family, adversity was about to be redefined. The decision to not wait another day in bringing Conor home would prove to be life-saving in the ultimate way.

☙ chapter 27 ☙

My mom was notoriously positive. I really cannot recall a time she did not see the potential for good to rise in any situation. When I was young, it was really annoying. As a whining teenager, there were times I just didn't want to do something, like work an 8-hour shift serving ice cream to youth soccer teams at the local ice cream store. Let's just say it was a challenge each Saturday afternoon when I was assigned to an elongated table of 10-year-old soccer players, each of whom was eager for their custom-made ice cream treat. Keeping track of ice cream flavors with personalized toppings for a party of 15 was, at times, mind-boggling. I realize it's all about the details, but after I dropped a chocolate milk shake on a coach's lap, the toils of the job got to me.

"Give it up for someone," my mom used to say when I really didn't want to go to work. Her enduring signature message was to stretch her children's short-sighted vision to the world beyond the tendency for tunneled existence. Inherently, she was tuned in to those less fortunate in possession or affection. When young, inevitably my siblings and I would roll our eyes at her unwillingness to meet us in our poutiness. I realized later when I said the same thing to my own children that my mom's outlook of outreach never validated our adolescent self-centeredness. Her tactics, however, never felt like the tough love of "get yourself to work NOW." Instead, always with understanding, she laid down the gauntlet with compassion, inclusivity, and optimism. Her reminders that the enclosed room of our own lives existed within a vast mansion of grander stories opened our perspective. She infused fresh air no matter how trite or profound the experience. Nothing ever worked well if we made it about ourselves. Over time, I realized I wanted to be just like her.

My second pregnancy ended in a miscarriage. Our firstborn, Kate, was 18 months at the time. I was devastated. Compounded by medical complications following our loss, my mom came to spend a few days with me as I recovered. Many friends and family members offered their sympathies. Many meant well, but their attempts at consolation left me with a lesson in what not to say to others who suffer similar loss.

"At least you have Kate…"

"You'll have another child…"

"At least you weren't farther along in your pregnancy."

The circuitous attempts to make me feel better didn't address the loss of this child I wanted so much. My grief was real and not so easily dismissed by "at least." It was a difficult time for me.

In the immediate days following my loss, my mom draped cool compresses on my tear-weary eyes and prepared tea and toast to nourish my lost appetite. She offered words of encouragement that allowed the possibility that life would carry on, and joy would rise again. The baby I lost, she told me, would pave the way to new life. And it did. "You are strong and healthy," she told me, "and you will heal." And I did. "Think about all those who have lost a child," she added, "because now you can understand and offer compassion born from knowing."

She was right. Here was a woman who had forged ahead in life despite the most heartbreaking death of Pat, not to mention her loss of Thomas, who was never offered a chance at life. As my mom nurtured my broken heart, she did so with her signature positivity. The tender touch of her weathered hands gave proof that life goes on. The compassionate look from her wrinkled eyes reminded me that love rises even from heartache. And the inevitable run in her panty hose reminded me that life isn't perfect. Sometimes things happen without a good reason, but good rises anyway. Never could I have imagined how my mom's uncanny ability to offer comfort would be tested even more than the day of Conor's injury.

* * * * *

I was in Bloomington, Indiana visiting Kate and her family the night Conor and Phil arrived in Dayton. I had been in touch with Kathy by text and knew the depth of her relief in having both of them home. She looked forward to rebuilding Conor's physical and mental stamina by healthy nutrition and lots of rest. There is nothing like being enveloped by the care of a loving mom. I went to bed grateful for my sister's peace of mind.

I was sleeping in my daughter's guest room after a busy day of princess play and swing-set fun. It had been a stormy evening in Indiana, and I remember the startle of thunderous booms throughout the night awakening me from sleep.

In the still, dark hour of the early morning, the melodic ringtone of my cell phone interrupted my slumber. Caller ID indicated it was my sister.

"Kath?" I said, unnerved by her call. There had been way too much post-traumatic stress from these early morning phone calls.

Her voice was quivering. "We're all okay," she said, "But Anne, our house was struck by lightning and is on fire."

*What? Say that again? You have **got** to me kidding me.* After all my sister had endured, now her house was on fire? I couldn't find any words to console her. Nothing. My feeble attempts to say anything to Kathy fell into an abyss of worthlessness. All I could say was, "I'm on my way."

Once again, in the darkness of the night, the intrusion of catastrophe left me in shock. Did I really just hear from my sister that her house was burning? I was encased in utter disbelief. I had to process what I'd just heard. *My sister's house was on fire.* The thought of violent flames destroying my sister's home left me gasping for breath.

I left Kate a note on her kitchen counter and set out before dawn for the three-hour drive home. I gripped the steering wheel to navigate the wet, windy roads. Attempting to corral my internal bedlam, I became consumed by anger.

"Where were you?" I cried out in the car. My voice cracked with hysteria. I was screaming to God, my mom, my brothers and every other heavenly being who I believed had a front row seat in the game of choreographing life. How could this have happened? Where was the fairness? How could two catastrophic life events happen to the same family? Honestly, how many families experience a traumatic brain injury and home destruction by fire in one lifetime. It made no sense, and I found no words to describe the confusion, unfairness, and cruelty of this fate. I felt even more outraged than the early days following Conor's accident. I had been such a soldier of faith for my sister and believed Conor's recovery was divinely orchestrated, but the fact that her house was ablaze was just too much. My sister had been a steward of trust in God's touch and abundant grace that propelled her to each new day with hope; but her days were anything but easy. And now this? I felt for the first time, even as my mother's daughter, there was no good left. This was just too much.

I envisioned the vicious ruin of her home, and felt as if that thread of commitment to the greater spiritual story was severed.

This was just wrong, and my arsenal of emotional potency was spent. All I could do was scream in disbelief.

I called Gerry who immediately went to be with Kathy. I called my dearest friends pleading with them to step in for me until I could get home. The drive left me in isolation with my anger and resentment to the same God I had entrusted the care of my sister.

I arrived home as the extensive destruction was settling in. Entering my house, I found my kitchen had been transformed by our very own team of first responders. Boxes of bagels and cardboard containers of hot coffee lined my kitchen counters. Gerry, his wife Kristen and my friends stood, offering the kind of priceless comfort offered by those who aren't afraid to show up. Barely saying hello to anyone, I simply asked, "Where is she?"

I found my sister exiting the bathroom with a pile of smoke-filled clothes in her arms. The scent of burn lingered. Kristen's early morning shopping trip to Walmart gave the gift of simple relief: clean clothes and a toothbrush. Kathy and I embraced. Unlike the lobby of Illinois Masonic, there was nothing to say. I felt her defeat. Her sobs reverberated through the emptiness of my ability to offer any words. This was simply unbelievable.

Shepherding her back to my kitchen, all present pulled up chairs and we sat at the kitchen table. The enveloping support was tangible in the calm amidst the chaos. As my sister's world was literally burning to the ground, those of us who gathered around my kitchen table did what we'd always done as family. We offered comfort in worldly ways, like a toasted bagel or cup of hot tea. Tears flowed. There we heard the story. As I heard my sister talk, my desperate anger turned to a shivering "what if?"

Kathy began.

Phil and Conor arrived home from Chicago around 10 pm the night before. The evening storms were gaining strength, but they paid little attention. Kathy was so relieved to have them home. She offered a quick late-night dinner and sent Conor off to bed for much-needed rest.

Sometime around 4:30 a.m., a violent, earsplitting strike of lightning reverberated throughout their home, waking them with a start. Arising to check on Conor, Kathy noticed a small, slight patch of singed carpet near the foot of his bed where the metal air vent met the rug. Initially, there was no cause for alarm. Nothing else seemed troubling. As a precaution, however, Phil thought it best to give the house a look. Before returning to bed, he stepped outside. Exiting his front door, he turned and looked up toward the roof. Flames were shooting from the attic above Conor's bedroom.

"GET OUT," Phil screamed from the lawn. "GET OUT!"

Phil ran back inside the house, frantically grabbing the collection of important family documents.

A moment of panic has a million particles. Kathy screamed to Conor. She ran downstairs to grab her purse, car keys, and Conor's anti-seizure medication. She went to the stairs again calling him, yelling at him.

"Conor," she screamed. "Conor!"

"Ma, I'm outside," he yelled directly through the pandemonium.

Kathy turned towards the open front door. There, on the front lawn was Conor in his shorts and t-shirt holding both of their dogs. He'd made it out first.

Wearing pajamas, robe, and bedside slippers, Kathy, Conor, and the dogs were able to take her car from their burning home intact. Her heart GPS took them to my driveway, where she called me.

Phil remained as firefighters worked to smother the flames eviscerating his home. For the next several hours he watched as water logged their house, dousing a lifetime of mementos, photographs, and tangibles that constitute a home. Their cul-de-sac was thick with smoke, making the attempt to salvage anything futile.

I pondered the whereabouts of God, but as I listened to my sister once again stalled by misfortune, I heard a story supported by a gratitude greater than anything I'd ever experienced. Clarity thawed my anger. The realization that this tragedy was just one degree from even greater devastation left me shaking. Revisiting the events of the night left me overcome with *what if.* I couldn't even process what I was hearing.

If life had proceeded as "expected," Conor would have been in Chicago that night. Because he was home, the violent crack of thunder caused Kathy and Phil to get out of bed to check on him. Otherwise, they would have turned over and gone back to sleep, just like I did in Kate's guest bed. The firefighter told Phil that because the fire engulfed the attic space first, the smoke detectors probably would not have activated in time for them to get out of the house safely.

"Your son being home saved your lives," the fireman said. The realization that their lives had been spared so tenuously left me paralyzed with the possibility that we could have lost much more than their home. I heard my mom's words. *Be grateful.*

We sat at my kitchen table for hours. Friends and family remained with us, offering an all-day embrace. Realizations that this destruction could have been even worse became clear. Phil, Kathy, Conor and the dogs were alive and well. Small miracles continued to emerge. The firefighters found Kathy's wedding ring and they removed from the house our parent's wedding album, remarkably untouched. Although clothes, furniture and the majority of their possessions were unsalvageable, certain finds caused us to cheer with gratitude. My mom's Royal Daulton figurines, our grandmother's china and few pieces of heirloom jewelry were somehow intact. Every time Phil called with a found relic, we celebrated with renewed appreciation for its meaning. We gave each other high-fives as if we'd won the lottery over and over again.

Casseroles, sandwiches, fruit plates, and offers to "do anything" were in constant flow from friends who streamed through the revolving kitchen door. They too, had no words as they hugged Kathy, Phil, and Conor. This catastrophic house fire felt so random and senseless. The only thing to do was offer a chair, some lasagna, and a place at our table. We laughed, we cried, we cursed and we wondered. Once again, the best of life rose to the top of tragedy because people offered hope and love. There were still no answers, but at least we were together. The scenarios of possibilities lingered; only one degree of difference between devastation of their home and irreplaceable loss of life. I couldn't rest in that place long. Imagining life without them was just not fathomable.

There was a poetic flow of the day of the fire which mirrored the rhythm of Conor's recovery. Amidst calamity, there was the allowance of celebration which allowed Kathy and Phil to thread joy into grief and anguish. The golden triumph in watching Conor put his life back together cultivated an appreciation and value for life they could have never otherwise comprehended. Once again, the Crippens were thrust into the tomb, where destruction could have threatened belief in hope and resurrection. By now, however, they were Crippen strong. Wisdom born from their grounded choices to love and hope kept them from crumbling amidst the ashes. They knew the bricks and mortar of a house had nothing to do with a home. Since Conor's accident, home meant they were together; all five of them.

Listening to Conor's reaction to the fire was like sitting in an oasis in the middle of a vast desert. He offered what he always did, perspective with humor.

"This is quite an unfortunate way to begin a day," he said, followed by his signature grin and wrapping of arms around his mom's shoulders.

With everyone sitting around my kitchen table, Conor was asked the big question we were all grappling with.

"Why do you think this happened?"

In his Dalai Lama sort of way, he paused. He was in no hurry to answer as he collected his thoughts.

"Do you want the scientific answer or the spiritual answer?" He responded with soft and seasoned eyes. This wasn't his first rodeo in placing misfortune into a greater good. He went on to describe the perfect storm of scientific explanation that may have contributed to a lightning strike on their house, the only one in the neighborhood. He spoke of water, electrical currents and how the position of the house could have led to the accidental fire.

"And as for the spiritual reason?" he added with his hands clasped and resting gently on his lap. "It's to remind us of the impermanence of things." He said. His words were soft and thoughtful. I was moved to tears at his knowing, his insight, and his ability to connect the awfulness of hardship with transcending wisdom. But I wasn't surprised. I had been witness to this filter through which Conor views life. Since his accident, optimism, goodness, and promise defined his entire outlook—even amidst TBI recovery. We all sat in silence. Conor sees optimism, goodness, and promise in everything.

However, the most poignant realization was the memory of the RIC physician counseling Kathy and Bridget that fateful day two months after Conor's accident.

"You will never be able to leave him home alone. He won't know what to do if the house catches on fire."

Literally, it took a fire, but the fact that Conor was the first out of the house with his dogs turned to mush all previous projections of limited recovery.

Although this house fire left questions and shook the fragile trust the Crippens had cultivated following Conor's devastating accident, I knew they could rebuild. The only way this made sense to me, however, was to think that maybe, just maybe the burning of their home was the only way to start a new life not defined by Conor's accident. Up to this point, the heavy burden of Conor's rehabilitation consumed all energy, and their home embodied tangible evidence of his progress post-accident. His bedroom had become a shrine of healing. Covering the walls were charts, calendars, and reminders marking the extensive devotion to restore his mind. In their basement were boxes that held thousands of pages of Conor's extensive medical records from Advocate Illinois Masonic Hospital. Now, it was all unrecognizable amidst the massive pile of ashes that lay quiet against the concrete foundation of their house. They had no choice but to start over in everything.

Maybe I channeled my mom a bit too much that day, but I was overcome with gratitude. The embers of their home were still smoldering, but I couldn't help but rejoice in my relief that my sister and her family were present and unharmed sitting within my arms' reach.

"You can rebuild," I told her.

"Think about all those who lose their homes to tornados or hurricanes," I told her.

"At least you're all okay," I said through grateful tears.

In hindsight, Kathy probably wanted to test her pie throwing skills again, but I didn't allow much time to drown in despair as we spent the day sitting around the kitchen table. I was too grateful her family was unharmed. Mourning the grandness of their loss would come in the days ahead as they picked through the rubble of a former life. But that day, sitting around my kitchen table offered a cocoon of strength garnered from the gathering of those who simply showed up. We toasted to the good that was already rising from the literal ashes.

Now faced with irreparable damage of almost everything they owned, Kathy and Phil's attitude didn't rest too long in gloom. My sister and her family had faced the mourn of tragedy before. The road of Conor's healing taught them what was really important in life. Their son defied the odds. They almost lost him in the aftermath of a senseless accident, but they didn't. The journey of healing and restoration was about focus and intentional rebuttal of any sort of victim-like response. No longer did they sweat the small stuff. A speeding ticket couldn't ruin the day. Airline flight delays were met with a shoulder shrug and an opportunity to chat with other stranded passengers. And if the Thanksgiving turkey was way overcooked? Well, that's what gravy was for.

The house fire was another reminder that "life" isn't really in the business of evenhandedness. Yes, my sister and her family have suffered from more catastrophic events than one family should. Although we know that it's rare for someone to traverse life unscathed by challenge, the fact that my sister has had to endure such intense hardship and loss certainly begs head-scratching. The reality, though, is that others are called to endure the heavy tipped scale of hardships as well. Some people survive one type of cancer only to be diagnosed with another. Some people mourn the loss of children only to lose yet again. And then there are those who find themselves affected by random acts of violence where there is little good to be found. Kathy and her family don't own the patent on pain, but somehow, they figured out how to forge ahead guided by love. Surrounded by the wreckage and ruin of material importance, they would hold on tight to their family unit of support. I was reminded of the words I wrote after attending the Kripalu writer's workshop just months following Conor's accident.

It is not forever that we will be "living in" the aftermath of Conor's accident. There will be a time when we will "bring with" his story to a greater tapestry.

✲ chapter 28 ✲

The Crippens did rebuild. They now live in a new home that is symbolic of a new life. No longer defined exclusively by the circumstances of Conor's injury, they are all seeking revamped joys. Bridget is blissfully married to a man who never knew Conor before his accident, and it doesn't matter. The intense years of pain that came to feel like a status quo of struggle have been gracefully replaced by a new paradigm of living. Bridget is scheduled to graduate with a Doctorate in Psychology. Her dissertation is a study illuminating the impact of the autism spectrum on siblings. Her emphasis on how children are effected when a brother or sister navigates a compromised normalcy is a direct concequence of her own journey alongside her brother. Jack is enrolled as a graduate student at Xavier University in Cincinnati. He is pursuing a Master's Degree in Hospital Administration. Jack wishes to be part of the system which has the potential to offer restoration and healing to others. No longer bearing responsibilities greater than anticipated, he is able to live within the freedom of his own dreams. Bridget and Jack have been profoundly impacted by Conor's fate. Instead of turning away from their brother's unwelcome journey, they chose to remain with their parents in the thick of it; observing and participating in the quest to restore Conor to wellness. They paid attention, and have chosen life careers in direct response to their experiences and scrutiny as siblings.

Far too young, Bridget and Jack were called to bravery, courage, and level of faith required to help Conor thrive amidst doubt. They both have woven into their young lives determination and tenacity ingrained through the importance of family.

As for Kathy and Phil? These days, they are in the business of new discoveries. Lingering lunches, travel dreams come true, and spur-of-the-moment weekend getaways flow from their enjoyment in being together. I never quite know where Sunday fun-days will take them. Kathy now shares her story of creative problem solving in brain rehabilitation and its broader relevancy in education. At the request of the Centerville School District, she has presented to fellow teachers the lessons she's learned as a mother how to cultivate new pathways of her son's mind. I can only imagine how many young students have been directly impacted by the expansion of Kathy's professional palate. Her hope is that others might benefit from Conor's remarkable example of how to rewire brain function. As she shares her own unique message of how to cope with unwelcome tragedy, she combines traditional thinking with resourceful quests that leaves others inspired, even when immersed in despair or brokenness. She speaks to the larger, universal themes of where to search for promise and hope. For those who feel they have been bombarded by excessive trial, Kathy's example of endurance and recognition of gratitude helps propel movement; where one step at a time offers trust that struggle will yield something positive. As her platform continues to expand, I sit back and wait—brimming with the pride of an older sister—knowing that her reach will grow beyond anything she could have imagined.

Conor spent a year living independently in Vancouver, Canada where he participated in a full-time therapy program with the Watson Centre for Brain Health. Designed to unlock even more of his higher brain function, Conor's accomplishment in living on his own and navigating life with increased creativity has left him poised for abundant living. I think back to the very first PRFC post logged just hours after Conor's injury. In it, I wrote,

> "Conor will return to the world all he has been given in hope and faith."

I have a front row seat to Conor's life. Does he have lingering effects of his brain injury? Yes. Short term memory requires him to still use his iPhone calendar and reminders to navigate the details of living. That right arm tremor is still a nuisance. Still to be revealed is a path for him that will meet and extend the triumphant recovery following a catastrophic accident. More meaningful, however, is the impact I see him have with others. Tenderness, ability to listen, and an awareness refined by the unique challenges thrust upon him dictate his perspectives. Despite his youth, wisdom has taken residence in the way he extends himself to others. I see people relax into Conor's presence, realizing his perspectives come from sacred space. Insight seeps through his words, his thoughts, and how he expresses himself. His message is uplifting, hopeful and always leaves others feeling good about the world. His charisma is infectious. I have no doubt he will continue to imprint the world with his charm, wit, and ability to connect deeply with people. Conor makes brain injury accessible, and his signature way of not taking himself too seriously is a lesson we can all learn from. In a recent blog post of his own, Conor wrote the following.

August 14, 2019

What's up everybody. It's been a bit since my last post to you guys and I would like to post about some of the experiences

I have had of late; embarrassing experiences but ones that have to be reacted to with a little humor. So, I was taking a class at Wright State University this summer. I have a lot of credits to catch up on because I was pretty behind where I am supposed to be. Long story short, I locked my car right before I went into my class. After my class I was trying to find my car and was confused when my key wasn't unlocking my car. I kept trying and trying until finally I called campus security to help me out. They came and unlocked the car. No problem. Immediately after I looked inside (the car) and my heart sank in embarrassment. I realized the car we had just "broken into" was actually not my car at all. I looked at the guard with an embarrassed expression, and said, "Sh%#, I don't think this is my car?!?" We both looked at each other, eyes wide and a smirk appeared on her face. Ironically, my car was actually 10 feet away and thankfully my key worked just fine. Fortunately, I was able to drive it away chuckling to myself for my mistake. From what I learned, we are all going to have extremely embarrassing moments and that doesn't make you weird or abnormal (Just don't go breaking into other peoples' cars or anything). You know in all of those situations no matter how embarrassing it is sometimes all you can do is chuckle at the situation you were placed in. I know that every situation is not a laughing matter, but just to keep your mood and outlook positive. It's the only thing we have, the ability to laugh or chuckle. Might I add, we all have to find the humor or the glass half full, no matter what. It's a better alternative.

Good is rising.

. . . . .

One of my favorite authors is Sue Monk Kidd. In her book, *When the Heart Waits*, she writes, "We seem to have focused so much on exuberant beginnings and victorious endings that we've forgotten about the slow, sometimes tortuous, unraveling of God's grace that takes place in the 'middle places.'"

It's been almost seven years since Conor was randomly hit by a speeding car on a downtown Chicago street. The desperate plea for the road whispered in my ear that morning in the lobby of a hospital would begin a journey for my sister she never could have envisioned—nor could I. Having been by her side I can assure you that none of this has been easy. Still, her sustaining energy was a choice to be led by something greater than her doubt and pain. I realize that the foundation cemented by our mom's model of how to live is why Kathy prevailed. Her scars continue to heal even after all this time, easily ripped open sometimes in unexpected ways. Kathy's perseverance, however, offers an example for our minds and hearts when in a state of awareness. Each day can stretch us to greater growth and understanding, far beyond what we thought we were capable of.

Kathy's innate yearning to walk a path with intention has been tough, but tortuous unraveling of grace began long before Conor's accident. The serendipity of wonder, similar to a hummingbird's ability elevate a troubled mind, has been part of our Grogan story all along. Navigating our loss of Pat, reconciling the brokenness of our parents' marriage, the call to care for our mom and the subsequent death of Neil all taught us the value of remaining where we don't want to be. We've been challenged more than once to carve a new path in the course of struggle. For Kathy, her son's fluke accident called her to rise above herself in the ultimate way.

Our best lessons in how to live came from our mom's robust grip and her reminders to look towards the sky for delight. No one did the "middle place" better than my her. Kathy knew that too. Gerry was right when he reminded Kathy on a particularly difficult day that she embodied a capacity to hope just like our mom. Still, the summon is far from easy.

Love of spirit-fragmented brothers gave us an appreciation for how souls can erode within lonely isolation. Kathy learned, by Pat's and Neil's examples, to remain in light despite her pain. Her partnership with Phil offered a safe place to rest her weary heart, and the outreach of thousands through Facebook encouraged her with hopeful intention. I like to think my brothers extended their heavenly touch in delicate ways. Perhaps when a warm breeze tickled her cheek, Pat and Neil were giving their little sister a loving embrace, reminding her she was stronger than she thought. Their legacies have been tattooed on the hearts of Gerry, Kathy, and me. We remain Grogan strong because of them.

As for our sisterhood? Kathy and I have traveled many roads together. My sister's resolute quest to bring Conor "home" following his catastrophic brain injury was born from a lifetime of fortitude. Together, we have been gifted with the ability to rise up time and time again. That fateful night in March 2013, however, sentenced me to a new role. Unable to share her heavy yoke, I could only be alongside Kathy, offering the surety of our sisterhood. My love and admiration for my sister reaches beyond the moon's horizon. If you'd ask Kathy, I'm sure she'd say she couldn't have done it without me. It's probably true, because one thing I know for sure is that when we walk arm in arm, we can do anything. I pray for Kathy to experience more ordinary time and ability to revel in a more relaxed realm in the "middle place." I pray that moving forward, her life terrain has a bit less gravel, and wider room for contentment. Either way, we will continue to journey together, grateful we have one another to walk the road we've been given.

July 4, 2017 PRFC

I've learned and experienced a lot. My desire to experience more has greatly increased. I feel empowered and ready for more challenges to exceed limits that were once, and may still be, placed on me. I wish for everyone that life continues to go well. Thanks for reading. ~ Conor

with gratitude

Writing this book stretched me in a multitude of ways. The most difficult task was overcoming my own insecurities and frequent self-doubt. Without the inspiration and expertise of the following people, I would have no doubt crawled into the hole of discouragement. When the disconnect between the final chapter and what to do next hit me, Todd Romer empowered me to reach out and make a plan for fruition. I placed my initial vulnerability into the hands of Wendy Nikolai who, with gentleness and honesty, was the first to read and edit this story. She provided unmeasurable encouragement which propelled me to carry on. Others offered their honest critique: Kate Ratliff, Bridget Jones, Carol Nikolai and Carleen Suttman. My constant cheerleaders were Denise O'Connell, Cathy Girmann, Jiffie Hart and Debbie McGraw. I am indebted to their frienship.

It was a serendipitous moment one summer afternoon – my niece Beth Romer and I shared a glass of wine on the deck of our lake house in Eaton, Ohio. She and I already had a bond grounded in mutual love and admiration. But, when she said to me, "I'll help you," with regard to my vision, the process of finishing this book was energized and laced with her creative marketing direction. Who knew Beth and I would forge ahead together sharing a belief that this story needed to be told. Through Beth, I have come to appreciate Megan Jakubs who takes care of my cyber world.

I am grateful to Emily Bonistall-Postel, whose professional expertise gave me the final push towards completion. This process has left me enriched by such talented people. This team makes my heart swell in gratitude.

When the dream of publication was in sight, I turned towards my niece Brandie Grogan for artistic input. My trust in her ability to come up with just the right cover came from a lifetime of knowing and loving her. Her gentle spirit, incredible talent, and ability to translate a compilation of this big story into a simple cover design made everything feel right. I'm so happy to have loved her every day of her life.

I'm grateful to my Grogan family, and especially my brother Gerry just because he makes you feel like anything is possible. Kathy will forever be my life partner, and the vibrant spirits of our Mom and brothers Pat and Neil provided inspiration when my writing well felt dry. My dad's example of what it means to belong to a family continues to ignite appreciation for our ability to be there for one another.

I would be nothing without the love of my children, Kate, Ben, Matthew and Holly. But most of all, I'm thankful for my husband Mark for giving me the space and occasional push I needed to get this labor of love complete.

Conor Crippen's courage and perseverance connect every word of this story. He continues to inspire and live his message of hope. For today and every day, Go Conor Go.

about the author

Anne Marie is a writer inspired by family connection, grief, and fleeting serendipity. She articulates the language of the heart in a way which binds the human experience. She writes about the bliss of being a mom and grandmother and the angst of caring for elderly parents. She writes about the loss of her two brothers, Pat and Neil, to suicide in hopes that light can shine onto others who may be suffering from despair. She has become a suicide awareness advocate in her community.

Her essays highlight connections we can all relate to. She is a Community Contributor to the Dayton Daily News.

Anne Marie is propelled by the relentless quest to highlight good that rises even amidst debilitating pain. Her writings can be found at Annemarieromer.com.

Anne Marie lives outside Dayton, Ohio with her husband Mark.

CPSIA information can be obtained
at www.ICGtesting.com
Printed in the USA
BVHW031211260422
635362BV00009B/177